Looking Ahead at the Cybersecurity Workforce at the Federal Aviation Administration

Committee on Cybersecurity Workforce of the
Federal Aviation Administration

Board on Human-Systems Integration
Division of Behavioral and Social Sciences and Education

Computer Science and Telecommunications Board
Division on Engineering and Physical Sciences

A Consensus Study Report of

The National Academies of
SCIENCES · ENGINEERING · MEDICINE

THE NATIONAL ACADEMIES PRESS
Washington, DC
www.nap.edu

THE NATIONAL ACADEMIES PRESS   500 Fifth Street, NW   Washington, DC 20001

This activity was supported by contract number 692M15-19-T-00028 between the National Academy of Sciences and the Federal Aviation Administration. Any opinions, findings, conclusions, or recommendations expressed in this publication do not necessarily reflect the views of any organization or agency that provided support for the project.

International Standard Book Number-13: 978-0-309-39150-4
International Standard Book Number-10: 0-309-39150-4
Digital Object Identifier: https://doi.org/10.17226/26105

Additional copies of this publication are available from the National Academies Press, 500 Fifth Street, NW, Keck 360, Washington, DC 20001; (800) 624-6242 or (202) 334-3313; http://www.nap.edu.

Copyright 2021 by the National Academy of Sciences. All rights reserved.

Printed in the United States of America

Suggested citation: National Academies of Sciences, Engineering, and Medicine. 2021. *Looking Ahead at the Cybersecurity Workforce at the Federal Aviation Administration*. Washington, DC: The National Academies Press. https://doi.org/10.17226/26105.

The National Academies of
SCIENCES · ENGINEERING · MEDICINE

The **National Academy of Sciences** was established in 1863 by an Act of Congress, signed by President Lincoln, as a private, nongovernmental institution to advise the nation on issues related to science and technology. Members are elected by their peers for outstanding contributions to research. Dr. Marcia McNutt is president.

The **National Academy of Engineering** was established in 1964 under the charter of the National Academy of Sciences to bring the practices of engineering to advising the nation. Members are elected by their peers for extraordinary contributions to engineering. Dr. John L. Anderson is president.

The **National Academy of Medicine** (formerly the Institute of Medicine) was established in 1970 under the charter of the National Academy of Sciences to advise the nation on medical and health issues. Members are elected by their peers for distinguished contributions to medicine and health. Dr. Victor J. Dzau is president.

The three Academies work together as the **National Academies of Sciences, Engineering, and Medicine** to provide independent, objective analysis and advice to the nation and conduct other activities to solve complex problems and inform public policy decisions. The National Academies also encourage education and research, recognize outstanding contributions to knowledge, and increase public understanding in matters of science, engineering, and medicine.

Learn more about the National Academies of Sciences, Engineering, and Medicine at **www.nationalacademies.org**.

The National Academies of SCIENCES · ENGINEERING · MEDICINE

Consensus Study Reports published by the National Academies of Sciences, Engineering, and Medicine document the evidence-based consensus on the study's statement of task by an authoring committee of experts. Reports typically include findings, conclusions, and recommendations based on information gathered by the committee and the committee's deliberations. Each report has been subjected to a rigorous and independent peer-review process and it represents the position of the National Academies on the statement of task.

Proceedings published by the National Academies of Sciences, Engineering, and Medicine chronicle the presentations and discussions at a workshop, symposium, or other event convened by the National Academies. The statements and opinions contained in proceedings are those of the participants and are not endorsed by other participants, the planning committee, or the National Academies.

For information about other products and activities of the National Academies, please visit www.nationalacademies.org/about/whatwedo.

COMMITTEE ON CYBERSECURITY WORKFORCE OF THE FEDERAL AVIATION ADMINISTRATION

DIANA L. BURLEY, *Co-Chair,* American University
TONYA L. SMITH-JACKSON, *Co-Chair,* North Carolina A&T State University
RODNEY C. ADKINS, 3RAM Group
JANDRIA S. ALEXANDER, Booz Allen Hamilton
MARILYN BARRIOS, Motorola Solutions
CHARLES BLAUNER, Cyber Aegis; Team8 Ventures
MICHAEL D. COOVERT, University of South Florida
BARBARA ENDICOTT-POPOVSKY, University of Washington
ERIC GROSSE, Security Consultant
ROBERT S. GUTZWILLER, Arizona State University
KATYA LE BLANC, Idaho National Laboratory
NAN SHELLABARGER, FAA (Retired)

Staff

DANIEL TALMAGE, Co-Study Director
BRENDAN ROACH, Co-Study Director
ADAM JONES, Senior Program Assistant
TOBY WARDEN, Board Director, Board on Human-Systems Integration
JON EISENBERG, Board Director, Computer Science and Telecommunications Board
MONICA STARNES, Senior Program Officer, Transportation Research Board

BOARD ON HUMAN-SYSTEMS INTEGRATION

FREDERICK OSWALD, Department of Psychology, Rice University, *Chair*
JAMES BAGIAN (NAE/NAM), Institute for Healthcare Policy and Innovation, University of Michigan, Ann Arbor
DIANA BURLEY, Graduate School of Education and Human Development, George Washington University
BARBARA DOSHER (NAS), School of Social Sciences, University of California, Irvine
MICA ENDSLEY, SA Technologies, Mesa, Arizona
EDMOND ISRAELSKI, AbbVie, North Chicago, Illinois
JOHN LOCKETT, United States Army Research Laboratory (Retired)
NAJMEDIN MESHKATI, Viterbi School of Engineering, University of Southern California
EMILIE ROTH, Roth Cognitive Engineering, Stanford, California
WILLIAM J. STRICKLAND, Human Resources Research Organization, Alexandria, Virginia
MATTHEW WEINGER, Vanderbilt University Medical Center

Staff

TOBY WARDEN, Director

COMPUTER SCIENCE AND TELECOMMUNICATIONS BOARD

LAURA HAAS (NAE), University of Massachusetts, Amherst, *Chair*
DAVID CULLER (NAE), University of California, Berkeley
ERIC HORVITZ (NAE), Microsoft Corporation
CHARLES ISBELL, Georgia Institute of Technology
BETH MYNATT, Georgia Institute of Technology
CRAIG PARTRIDGE, Colorado State University
DANIELA RUS (NAE), Massachusetts Institute of Technology
FRED B. SCHNEIDER (NAE), Cornell University
MARGO SELTZER, University of British Columbia
NAMBIRAJAN SESHADRI, University of California, San Diego
MOSHE VARDI (NAS, NAE), Rice University

Staff

JON EISENBERG, Director

Preface

This report addresses the cybersecurity workforce challenges, and the strategic opportunities to meet those challenges, facing the Federal Aviation Administration (FAA) as it navigates the realities of modernization and an increasingly digitized National Airspace System (NAS). As the committee carried out its tasks, our knowledge and appreciation of the complexities associated with the FAA cybersecurity workforce has grown tremendously. The FAA is on par with other federal agencies in terms of the current capacity, capability, and diversity of its cybersecurity workforce. However, as the agency's digital footprint increases, their attack surface and vulnerability to outside threats will increase as well. The critical mission of the FAA necessitates that the agency strategically build a workforce that is able to meet both current and future needs.

The global demand for well-trained cybersecurity professionals in both industry and government continues to grow, and the tight labor market shows no signs of slowing. Given the strong demand, the FAA should simultaneously enact both short- and longer-term strategies to fill workforce needs. Fortunately, numerous opportunities exist for the FAA to grow the pool of available candidates and to develop capacity within their existing workforce. Through the varied recruitment and workforce development initiatives offered as recommendations throughout this report, the FAA can build a diverse pool of highly qualified candidates and strengthen workforce enhancement efforts.

We wish to express our deep appreciation to the members of the committee for their diligent and dedicated contributions. The committee's expertise and knowledge were indispensable throughout our deliberations. Their efforts, which often required working nights and weekends, are particularly notable given the incredibly challenging year. We cannot thank them enough. On behalf of the entire committee, we also wish to thank the National Academies of Sciences, Engineering, and Medicine staff for their outstanding support and guidance. We are also deeply appreciative to Heather Kreidler for her writing and fact checking. The report benefited deeply from the editing skills of Laura Yoder. Additionally, we want to express our sincere gratitude to everyone who contributed their time, expertise, and experiences to our committee. The presentations, resources, and insights contributed immensely to our deliberations. Finally, we wish to thank the FAA staff for their partnership and forthright participation throughout this process. We offer this report in the spirit of that partnership and believe that the concrete, actionable recommendations provided within will aid agency leaders as they continue to build the cybersecurity workforce and achieve their mission of providing the "safest, most efficient aerospace system in the world."

Diana Burley and Tonya Smith-Jackson, *Co-Chairs*
Committee on Cybersecurity Workforce of the Federal Aviation Administration

Acknowledgment of Reviewers

This Consensus Study Report was reviewed in draft form by individuals chosen for their diverse perspectives and technical expertise. The purpose of this independent review is to provide candid and critical comments that will assist the National Academies of Sciences, Engineering, and Medicine in making each published report as sound as possible and to ensure that it meets the institutional standards for objectivity, evidence, and responsiveness to the study charge. The review comments and draft manuscript remain confidential to protect the integrity of the deliberative process.

We thank the following individuals for their review of this report: Leisel Bogan, Congressional Digital Service Fellowship; David J. DeRosier, Department of Biology (emeritus), Brandeis University; Michael A. Echols, Max Cybersecurity LLC; R John Hansman, International Center for Air Transportation, Massachusetts Institute of Technology; Michael P. Huerta, MPH Consulting, LLC; Nani Lee, consultant, Waimea-South Kohala, Hawai'i; Michelle Monsees, consultant, Fairfax County, Virginia; Frederick L. Oswald, Department of Psychology, Rice University; and Juan Perez, United Parcel Service.

Although the reviewers listed above have provided many constructive comments and suggestions, they were not asked to endorse the conclusions or recommendations of this report nor did they see the final draft before its release. The review of this report was overseen by Jennie S. Hwang, H-Technologies Group, and Wesley L. Harris, Department of Aeronautics and Astronautics, Massachusetts Institure of Technology. They was responsible for making certain that an independent examination of this report was carried out in accordance with the standards of the National Academies and that all review comments were carefully considered. Responsibility for the final content of the report rests entirely with the authoring committee and the National Academies.

Contents

SUMMARY 1

1. INTRODUCTION 5
   Study Background, 5
   Charge to the Committee, 6
   Committee Approach, 7
   Report Structure and Summary, 9
   References, 9

2. CURRENT AND FUTURE CYBERSECURITY LANDSCAPE FOR THE
   FEDERAL AVIATION ADMINISTRATION 11
   The FAA, 11
      The FAA Mission, 11
      Organization and Structure of the FAA, 12
   The Cybersecurity Workforce of the FAA, 14
      The FAA's Current Cybersecurity Workforce, 14
      U.S. Cybersecurity Labor Market, 17
   FAA Employment Regulations, 17
      Statutory and Regulatory Requirements, 17
      Institutional Policies, 18
      Hiring, 18
      Retention, 21
      Contractors, 22
      The FAA's Future Cybersecurity Workforce, 22
   Summary, 23
      Conclusions and Recommendations, 23
   References, 24

3. MANAGING THE CAREER/EMPLOYEE LIFECYCLE FOR A DIVERSE
   CYBERSECURITY WORKFORCE   25
   Chapter Overview, 25
   Characteristics of the Cybersecurity Workforce in the 21st Century, 27
      Characteristics of the Cybersecurity Workforce, 27
      Cybersecurity Workforce Labor Market, 28
      Diversity in the 21st Century Cybersecurity Workplace, 28
   Recruitment and Hiring, 29
      Key Aspects of Recruitment, 29
      Key Asects of Selection, 30
      Cyber Aptitude Assessment, 32
      Federal Cyber Talent Development, 32
      Federal Recruitment, 33
      Federal Recruitment Flexibilities, 34
   FAA Recruitment and Hiring, 35
      Job Listings, 36
      Scholarship Opportunities and FAA Recruitment, 37
      Recruiting for Diversity in the FAA Cybersecurity Workforce, 38
   Development and Advancement, 39
      Reskilling and Training, 39
      Educational Conferences, 40
      Certification, 41
      Performance Management, 43
      Diversity and Inclusion in Organizational Culture, 45
   FAA Talent Development and Advancement, 45
      Reskilling and Training, 45
      Workforce Strategies and Best Practices, 46
      Development of Cybersecurity Awareness in Organizations, 46
      Coordination with Human Resources, 47
      Using the NICE Framework as a Guide to Identify Intense Personal Interest, 47
   Summary, 48
      Conclusions and Recommendations, 49
   References, 50

4. ADDITIONAL EMPLOYEE AND ORGANIZATIONAL CONSIDERATIONS   55
   Introduction, 55
   Retention, 55
      Compensation, 56
      Career Advancement and Development, 57
      Appreciation, 58
   FAA Retention, 58
      Human Capital in the Workplace, 59
      Focusing on Management Practices and Attitudes as Leading Indicators of Employee
         Intent to Depart from an Organization, 60
      Advancing Workplace Culture to Enhance Attractiveness of the Organization to Recruit
         and Retain Employees, 61
   Talent Pipeline Development, 62
      Early Training Talent Pipeline Development, 62
      College-Level Talent Pipeline Development, 63

CONTENTS   xv

        Diversity Through College-Level Talent Pipeline Development, 64
        Student-Level Talent Pipeline Development, 64
    FAA Talent Pipeline Development, 64
        Training, 65
        Skill Development and Training Through Certification, 66
        Workplace Flexibility, 66
    Retirement, 66
    Cybersecurity Organizational Stucture and Design, 67
        The CISO as a Senior Executive, 69
        CISO Independence, 69
        Three Lines of Defense, 69
        Hybrid/Federate First Line CISO Teams, 70
        Concluding Thoughts on Organizational Structure and Design, 71
    Summary, 71
        Conclusions and Recommendations, 71
    References, 72

5. KEY CHALLENGES AND OPPORTUNITIES   75
    Key Challenges, 76
    Key Opportunities, 77
    Reference, 79

APPENDIXES

A   Committee Meeting Agendas   83
B   Committee Biosketches   93

Summary

Section 549 of the Federal Aviation Administration Reauthorization Act of 2018 (P.L. 115-254) calls on the National Academies of Sciences, Engineering, and Medicine to examine the Federal Aviation Administration's (FAA's) cybersecurity workforce challenges, review the FAA's current strategy for meeting those challenges, and recommend ways to strengthen the FAA's cybersecurity workforce. Aspects under consideration include workforce size, quality, and diversity. This report provides the findings, conclusions, and recommendations of the National Academies' Committee on the Cybersecurity Workforce of the Federal Aviation Administration on these matters.

The FAA is responsible for providing the "safest, most efficient aerospace system in the world," as stated in its motto.[1] Over the past decade, it has overseen significant upgrades to the technology used to manage aviation operations to increase the safety and efficiency of the National Airspace System (NAS). Though necessary to regular operations, these modern computing and communications systems provide a greater attack surface for criminals, terrorists, or nation-states to exploit and thereby increase the potential for cybersecurity threats to the NAS and its constituents. Expanding digitization and connectivity *without adequate cybersecurity* could have enormous consequences; disruption anywhere in the aviation sector can spread across borders, cause significant financial damages, and compromise safety. While this transition is ongoing, the FAA still needs to protect its legacy-based systems.

The future safety and security of air travel will rely in part on the ability of the FAA to build a workforce capable of addressing the evolving cybersecurity threat landscape. Securing the computers, networks, and data that underpin modern aviation depends in part on the FAA having enough cybersecurity professionals (**capacity**) with the right knowledge, skills, and abilities (**capability**). It also depends on the FAA's workforce having sufficient **diversity** of backgrounds and experience. Such diversity is critical in analyzing cybersecurity problems and widely understood to be a "functional imperative" for effective cybersecurity programs.

The findings, conclusions, and recommendations contained herein derive from the academic literature, data received from the FAA, the committee's professional expertise, and input collected at the committee's five public meetings. Areas of professional expertise represented on this committee include relevant topical areas such as human capital management, organizational psychology, workforce diversity, industrial and systems engineering, and cybersecurity. Industry expertise was supplied by members who formerly served as senior managers of cybersecurity organizations. Government expertise was provided by a former deputy assistant administrator at the FAA.

---

[1] More information is available at: https://www.faa.gov/airports/central/about_airports/CE_mission/.

The five public meetings provided opportunities for the committee to learn about challenges and best practices from government and private-sector enterprises alike. The committee learned about challenges in other aviation enterprises (e.g., the European Union Aviation Safety Agency), major logistics and transportation corporations (e.g., UPS), and other government agencies (e.g., the Department of Education and the United States Coast Guard).

In the course of its work, the committee reached a number of findings, conclusions, and recommendations to guide the FAA's efforts. Chapters 2–4 of this report will present these along with supporting evidence and discussion. Chapter 5 reviews the committee's findings, conclusions, and recommendations. The findings, conclusions, and recommendations are summarized here in the form of key challenges and opportunities to ensure the FAA's cybersecurity workforce can continue to support the agency's missions. The committee notes that the FAA will need to recognize that these challenges and opportunities require constant evaluation and support by senior leadership.

KEY CHALLENGES

Challenge 1. Expansion of the FAA's digital footprint also increases vulnerability and risk, and so, increases the need for more robust cybersecurity due to these potential new threats. Cybersecurity is an essential element of fulfilling the agency's mission of ensuring safety in air travel. It has become a critical priority for the FAA, as risk is compounded by growing digitization and connectivity of the National Airspace System and aviation sector. As alluded to above, the increasing digitization of aviation infrastructure, while necessary to improve FAA operations, also expands the attack surface of critical infrastructure and cyber-physical systems. In response to these changing dynamics, the FAA will need to introduce a range of skills and expertise into its cybersecurity workforce.

Challenge 2. The cybersecurity labor market is highly competitive within the federal sector, nationally, and globally—and likely to become more so. Cybersecurity professionals are highly sought after, and competition among employers for the limited talent pool is likely to grow more acute. Despite a multitude of initiatives to address the cybersecurity workforce imperative, the nation still faces a significant shortage of qualified cybersecurity professionals. The demand for talent is particularly severe in the public sector, because federal agencies must compete with private-sector firms that often can provide better compensation. Compared to private employers, the FAA may not pay as highly but offers more stable employment and an attractive culture. It was noted in the committee's focus groups that there are instances where the FAA pay grades are above the rest of government for similar jobs and that this was an effective recruiting inducement. However, the FAA has further unique needs for its cybersecurity workforce, such as the need for employees who have a deep understanding of a highly specialized mission and technology infrastructure alongside an ability to defend against both cyber and security threats. Furthermore, the FAA will have to integrate cybersecurity professionals and cybersecurity practices into the agency's strong existing safety culture.

Challenge 3. The FAA faces a future wave of retirements in its cybersecurity workforce. Like many federal agencies, the FAA has a significant portion of employees who are or soon will be eligible for retirement. This means that within a relatively short timeframe, the FAA may have to replace a significant portion of its cybersecurity workforce amidst increasing competition for talent and ensure that the agency can retain the highly specialized, mission-specific knowledge of its retiring cybersecurity workforce.

Challenge 4. To achieve greater diversity within the cybersecurity workforce and meet its future needs, the agency must make better use of existing programs that promote workforce diversity. The FAA's diversity track record is on par with federal agencies and broader trends in terms of diversity of its workforce and its success in recruiting and retaining underrepresented minorities and women. But the FAA lags other parts of the federal government in taking advantage of existing programs for enhancing diversity. Increased diversity is vital to the FAA's future cybersecurity workforce for several reasons:

- Cybersecurity as a discipline incorporates a broad range of skills and knowledge, and thus an effective cybersecurity workforce will need to be diverse across a number of axes—a consideration that includes both

traditional diversity strategies, such as increased engagement of underrepresented minorities and women, and other strategies, such as encouraging applicants from a range of different educational institutions, previous employers, and geographic locations.
- Greater diversity represents an opportunity to grow the talent pool and anticipate changing national demographics. Growing this talent pool will allow the FAA to keep pace with other organizations that have made diversity a recruitment priority.
- Adversaries present a changing set of threat activities that challenge the imagination. To manage these tactics, a diverse and multiview cybersecurity defense is required as a critical part of the workforce.

Challenge 5. The FAA's current recruitment capabilities are not robust enough to meet future demand in an increasingly competitive environment. The FAA will need to be more effective in recruiting a cybersecurity workforce of sufficient capability and capacity in the face of worldwide competition for cybersecurity talent, the need to be ready to replace a wave of retirees, and the need for greater diversity in its cybersecurity workforce.

The challenges associated with building a diverse cybersecurity workforce of sufficient capability and capacity are in constant flux and under pressure as the FAA expands its digital footprint. It is the committee's hope that the opportunities summarized below and discussed in-depth in the rest of this report will help illuminate the steps that the FAA can take to strengthen its cybersecurity posture.

KEY OPPORTUNITIES

Opportunity 1. Leverage FAA's compelling mission as a recruitment tool. The FAA offers potential employees a work environment that combines cybersecurity operations with a unique mission (Finding 3-3). Through enhanced job fair materials, more compelling job descriptions, and engagements such as those identified in Opportunities 2-4, recruitment efforts can better highlight the opportunities to apply cybersecurity skills to the mission and within a unique operational environment (Finding 3-7).

Opportunity 2. Broaden the talent pipeline by building sustainable relationships with educational and industry partners and enhancing college recruitment. In order to help respond to the national imperative to grow the capability and capacity of the national and federal cybersecurity workforce and meet its own future needs, the FAA should consider investments in enriching educational curricula and scholarship programs and mining industry-based talent pools. A number of federal agencies have developed successful, replicable partnership activities that provide research opportunities, scholar-in-residence positions for federal cybersecurity practitioners, and student internships. Successful engagement can infuse the FAA with new cybersecurity talent. To realize this goal, the FAA will need to take full advantage of existing scholarship programs as well as explore new partnerships. The FAA should (1) evaluate the use of existing and future internship programs as a valuable tool to create a more diverse cybersecurity workforce (Recommendation 3-1); (2) organize and expand its reach and partnerships with universities around cybersecurity preparation efforts in academic and research areas in order to assist in the development of a talented cybersecurity workforce (Recommendation 3-3); and (3) set internal targets for the number of Scholarship for Service students recruited and/or hired to internships and permanent positions within the agency (Conclusion 3-5).

Opportunity 3. Enhance diversity by leveraging existing best practices. Other federal agencies have developed best practices that help to improve workforce diversity. For instance, several agencies have developed partnerships with minority serving institutions (MSIs),[2] similar to those discussed in Opportunity 2, that simultaneously attract young talent and improve organizational diversity. However, the FAA has not yet explored similar arrangements.

---

[2] The U.S. Department of Education's Minority-Serving Institutions Program includes the following organizations: Historically Black Colleges and Universities (HBCUs); Hispanic-Serving Institutions (HSIs); Tribal Colleges and Universities (TCUs); and Asian American and Pacific Islander-Serving Institutions (AAPISIs).

To address this shortfall, the FAA can (1) explore opportunities to develop meaningful and sustainable relationships with MSIs in order to access upcoming cybersecurity graduates via internships and employment opportunities (Recommendation 3-3); and (2) train its cybersecurity leadership on best practices in building a diverse and inclusive organizational culture (Recommendation 3-7).

Opportunity 4. Leverage federal hiring programs, nonsalary financial incentives, and flexibilities to attract and retain talent. Although subject to a number of requirements around federal hiring, the FAA could take better advantage of existing flexibilities, such as spot hiring authority (allowing employers to extend offers to qualified candidates without public posting requirements), which would allow it to more easily and nimbly recruit cybersecurity talent. While the FAA, like other federal agencies, cannot realistically hope to match the salaries of private-sector employers, the agency can better use certain nonsalary incentives such as increased quality of work-life balance and targeted geographic opportunities to compete for talent more effectively with other federal agencies. The FAA should compare its use of hiring flexibilities with those of other federal agencies, both highlighting currently existing flexibilities that are underused by the FAA and identifying other agency flexibilities and practices that could be incorporated into FAA hiring processes (Recommendation 2-4).

Opportunity 5. Promote and invest in training and reskilling. Given the wide range of skills relevant to its cybersecurity practice, reskilling current employees—including current cybersecurity staff, noncybersecurity information technology staff, and operations staff—can provide the FAA with a readily available talent pool of future cybersecurity talent. As the committee concluded, reskilling the existing workforce can be an important component of developing the needed future cybersecurity workforce of the FAA. To make best use of reskilling, the FAA should ensure that all efforts to upskill and evolve the cybersecurity workforce (Recommendation 3-5).

Opportunity 6. Anticipate the coming wave of retirements. The demographics of the FAA's cybersecurity workforce suggest that the agency will need to replace a significant portion of cybersecurity professionals in a relatively short timeframe. Although doing so will be challenging, the retirements also present an opportunity for FAA leadership to replace currently defined roles with ones that better reflect the future cybersecurity needs of the agency. To proactively address the challenges of anticipated retirements, the FAA should (1) implement cybersecurity workforce planning strategies that will protect the agency against the potential for sudden and mass retirements (Recommendation 2-1), and (2) provide professional development opportunities to refresh skill sets of current cybersecurity employees and ensure sharing of key institutional and mission-specific knowledge with newer cybersecurity staff (Recommendation 4-2).

Opportunity 7. Ensure that the FAA's chief information security officer (CISO) has sufficient authority and access to agency leadership. Mirroring private sector trends that have bolstered the role of CISOs, the FAA should consider providing the CISO role with more authority and access to agency leadership. This would allow the FAA to better identify and direct responses to cybersecurity challenges and foster an organizational culture in which cybersecurity professionals and other employees can be most effective in doing so. One option could be instituting a CISO's reporting structure to support a strong governance model, which ensures that the CISO has both the independence and access required to effectively manage the FAA's cyber risk posture (Recommendation 4-3).

1

Introduction

The mission of the Federal Aviation Administration (FAA) "is to provide the safest, most efficient aerospace system in the world."[1] In fulfilling this mission, the FAA faces significant cybersecurity challenges across its areas of responsibility, which range from air traffic control operations to aircraft safety certification. Underscoring the urgency of this challenge, a recent report by the National Academies of Sciences, Engineering, and Medicine concluded "the safety of life implications and the vital economic importance of air travel make the security of NextGen and the NAS (National Airspace System) critically important" (p. 9). The study conclusions urged the FAA to "strengthen its workforce in systems engineering and integration, digital communications, and cybersecurity" (NRC, 2015, p. 1).

It is against this backdrop of need and opportunity that the FAA requested the National Academies to conduct a subsequent study that specifically examines the cybersecurity workforce challenges and current strategy for meeting those challenges, so as to develop recommendations for enhancing that workforce. The cybersecurity workforce is composed of individuals in "work roles that have an impact on an organization's ability to protect its data, systems, and operations…. A cybersecurity workforce includes not only technically focused staff, but also those who apply knowledge of cybersecurity when preparing their organization to successfully implement its mission" (NIST, 2017, p. 1).

Using this broad conceptualization of the cybersecurity workforce, the resulting assessment reported herein incorporates a range of considerations intended to guide the FAA's ongoing efforts to strengthen the cybersecurity workforce and provides new recommendations for the future workforce development. The National Academies has performed similar studies for the FAA for modernizing the Air Traffic Control System and determining air traffic controller staffing needs (NRC, 2014, 2015). Additionally, the National Academies has studied ways to expand the professionalization of the cybersecurity workforce and foundational cybersecurity research strategies (NASEM, 2017; NRC, 2013).

STUDY BACKGROUND

This study attends to several challenges that may impact the continuation and future development of the FAA cybersecurity workforce. One broad challenge cited by many federal agencies and other organizations, including

---

[1] More information is available at: https://www.faa.gov/airports/central/about_airports/CE_mission/.

the FAA, is that cybersecurity talent is in high demand and short supply nationwide. It is notoriously difficult to quantify such shortages; there is, however, general agreement that the market for cybersecurity talent is tight. In a survey conducted by the Center for Strategic and International Studies (CSIS), 82 percent of employers reported a skills shortage in cybersecurity. Likewise, the same study indicated that 71 percent of employers believed the skill shortage impacts cybersecurity performance and effectiveness. The CSIS survey revealed a number of additional factors impacting the shortage of a skilled cybersecurity workforce (CSIS, 2016).

Exacerbating actual and perceived shortages is ongoing turnover, which is widespread in fast-moving high-tech fields even when there is an adequate number of qualified workers available, and especially when there is not (Business-Higher Education Forum, 2017; NRC, 2013). Other factors that any organization must consider when dealing with supply and demand challenges include recruitment, selection, performance assessment, levels of job variety and autonomy, promotion opportunities, management practices, and how to foster teamwork.

In the committee's judgment, supply and demand challenges are complicated by the way in which the field of cybersecurity integrates a variety of professions. Cybersecurity involves a range of professionals, from security architect to system administrator to personnel security manager, where the profiles of knowledge, skills, abilities, and interpersonal skills can vary significantly by profession. It also involves extensive collaboration with other professionals, such as when the operational implications of cybersecurity threats must be considered. Such variety must be considered when evaluating the complex cybersecurity challenges of the FAA and the workforce diversity enhancement efforts required to effectively address them. The cybersecurity workforce can be seen as a system in the context of recruiting, hiring, promoting, and retaining cybersecurity personnel. This system is complicated by the occupational breadth and independence of cybersecurity professionals.

Compared with the private sector (and federal agencies that have leveraged more flexible workforce management authorities), the FAA faces recruitment, training, and retention challenges reflecting factors, such as lower salaries; a highly specific and less cutting-edge technical environment; and citizenship, suitability, and security clearance requirements. On the other hand, many talented cybersecurity professionals work for federal agencies (Hernandez, 2020). Understanding why they chose this path and what obstacles to entry they faced may point to ways to improve recruitment and retention.

The FAA has been taking steps to address its cybersecurity workforce challenges. Recently it completed a transition from the old (computer specialist) to new (IT management) personnel series, thereby introducing much-needed cybersecurity specialties and making these positions more visible to job seekers (FAA, 2020). Recognizing its difficulty in competing for experienced cybersecurity talent, the agency has adopted a strategy emphasizing upskilling of its technical workforce to meet its cybersecurity needs. The present study looks at the effects these changes have had and considers more broadly how the job market and requirements of the field impact ongoing efforts to enhance cybersecurity in the FAA.

CHARGE TO THE COMMITTEE

The FAA sought the assistance of the National Academies to examine its cybersecurity workforce challenges and to develop new cybersecurity workforce recommendations. This request was a congressional requirement in Section 549 of the FAA Reauthorization Act of 2018 (P.L. 115-254). The specific charge from Congress to the FAA is shown in Box 1-1.

The committee's overall task was to examine the FAA's cybersecurity workforce challenges, review FAA's current strategy for meeting those challenges, and recommend ways to strengthen the FAA's cybersecurity workforce, including consideration of its size, quality, and diversity. Members of the committee represented expertise in related topical areas such as human capital management, industrial-organizational psychology, workforce diversity, industrial and systems engineering, and cybersecurity. For additional committee members, industry expertise was reflected in members who serve as senior managers of cybersecurity organizations, and former government employees. With regard to size, the committee considered the FAA's ability to meet current and anticipated future cybersecurity needs. In assessing the quality of the FAA's cybersecurity workforce, the committee sought to provide the FAA with recommendations to ensure the agency has enough cybersecurity workers (**capacity**) with the right knowledge, skills, and abilities (**capability**) (NRC, 2013). The committee took a similarly broad view of diversity

INTRODUCTION 7

> **BOX 1-1**
> **FAA Reauthorization Act of 2018**
>
> Section 549, of the 2018 FAA Reauthorization Act calls for a Study on the Cybersecurity Workforce of FAA and states that:
> (a) STUDY.—Not later than 1 year after the date of the enactment of this Act, the Administrator shall enter into an agreement with the National Academy of Sciences to conduct a study on the cybersecurity workforce of the Administration in order to develop recommendations to increase the size, quality, and diversity of such workforce, including cybersecurity researchers and specialists.
> (b) REPORT TO CONGRESS.—Not later than 180 days after the completion of the study conducted under subsection (a), the Administrator shall submit to the appropriate committees of Congress a report on the results of such study.

and used the Ford Foundation definition to position diversity as "the representation of all our varied identities and differences (race, ethnicity, gender, disability, sexual orientation, gender identity, national origin, tribe, caste, socio-economic status, thinking and communication styles, etc.), collectively and as individuals."[2] The committee was tasked with considering cybersecurity workforce needs across the FAA's mission areas and considering how these needs are likely to evolve. The evidence base, analysis, findings, conclusions, and recommendations will be discussed in more detail throughout the report. The committee's full statement of task is in Box 1-2.

COMMITTEE APPROACH

It was necessary to structure an appropriate committee to achieve the study goals and collect information on the scope and complexity of the FAA's cybersecurity workforce challenges, review the FAA's current activities for managing these challenges, and develop conclusions, findings, and recommendations that were responsive to the statement of task. To perform this task, the National Academies formed a committee of members with relevant expertise across a wide range of domains. The committee comprised 12 members, including two co-chairs. Specific expertise was provided on industrial-organizational psychology; human resource management (with emphasis on IT workers and related industries); diversity and inclusion; workforce development, staffing, and training; workforce systems; cybersecurity; cybersecurity education; computer and information science and engineering; software and information technology systems; and labor and workforce projections for cybersecurity. The committee was drawn from industry, the FAA, academia, and consulting organizations.

The committee's approach to its charge consisted of a review of the evidence in the scientific literature and several other information-gathering activities. In reviewing the literature and formulating its conclusions and recommendations, the committee considered all the presentations, literature searches, and committee knowledge.

The committee also held open public information-gathering sessions, which occurred through five planned meetings between February and November 2020. These meetings covered data accumulation and development of findings and recommendations, with the balance moving from former to latter as the meetings unfolded. The original intent for meetings two and three was to hold site visits, but due to the COVID-19 pandemic, all the committee's meetings were held virtually except meeting one. These data-gathering sessions included speakers from the FAA, other comparable organizations and agencies, airport representatives, and experts in cyber staffing, management, and organization. The FAA sponsor staff attended these open sessions to hear the information

---

[2]Definition taken from Ford Foundation; available at: https://www.fordfoundation.org/about/people/diversity-equity-and-inclusion/#:~:text=Diversity%20is%20the%20representation%20of%20all%20our%20varied,and%20communication%20styles%2C%20etc.%29%2C%20collectively%20and%20as%20individuals.

> **BOX 1-2**
> **Statement of Task**
>
> Pursuant to Section 549 of the FAA Reauthorization Act of 2018, a National Academies consensus study committee will (1) examine the Federal Aviation Administration's (FAA's) cybersecurity workforce challenges, (2) review the FAA's current strategy for meeting those challenges, and (3) provide recommendations related to strengthening the FAA's cybersecurity workforce, including consideration of its size, quality, and diversity. The study will consider cybersecurity workforce challenges agency-wide, including in such major functional areas as National Airspace System management, enterprise computing and communications infrastructure, air traffic control system acquisition and modernization, unmanned aircraft systems, and safety regulation. The study will take into account how the FAA's cybersecurity workforce needs are likely to change over time.
>
> Areas to be explored include the following:
>
> - The current and future cybersecurity landscape for the FAA and its mission areas;
> - Management and human resource approaches and strategies to achieve current and future desired outcomes that meet cybersecurity workforce needs, including recruitment and flexibilities, selection, retention, training, education, certification, and compensation considerations;
> - Cybersecurity organization structure, workforce strategies, and best practices of other government and private sector organizations with relevant missions, including air traffic management and aviation safety assurance;
> - Statutory, regulatory, and other institutional constraints on recruitment and flexibilities, hiring, retention, and compensation of cybersecurity workers;
> - Strategies to strengthen the cybersecurity workforce by attracting and retaining candidates from diverse backgrounds, including age, race, gender, and geography;
> - FAA organizational structure, culture, and norms that affect the cybersecurity workforce;
> - The U.S. labor market in cybersecurity expertise and commercial competition for qualified candidates; and
> - The existing structure used by the FAA to define the diverse set of workforce cyber knowledge, skills, and abilities, and its alignment with frameworks such as the National Initiative for Cybersecurity Education.
>
> The committee's evidence base, analysis, findings, conclusions, and recommendations will be set forth in a final report.

received by the committee, and to learn of the cybersecurity workforce challenges and opportunities to address them that other organizations employ. The committee also heard from multiple presenters on both the importance of and strategies for building and maintaining diversity in the workforce. The range of factors that define the diversity of an ideal workforce has been described in other settings as providing "the social context of decision making," wherein "diversity facilitates friction that enhances deliberation and upends conformity (Levine et al., 2014)." The social context of decision making at any organization demands that a broader conception of diversity is taken into account in the recruitment and hiring process.

Based on the range of information gathered during those meetings, the committee decided to explicitly define diversity for this report as found in Box 1-3.

BOX 1-3
Committee Definition of Diversity

The committee considers diversity to include, in the context of the Federal Aviation Administration's workforce needs, both the broad array of characteristics generally associated with diversity such as race, ethnicity, sexual orientation, and gender, as well as less frequently considered factors that shape an individual's identity. These other factors include, but are not limited to, geographical, national, academic, institutional or military affiliation, socioeconomic status, and linguistic background.

REPORT STRUCTURE AND SUMMARY

The report is divided into five chapters. The current chapter provides an overview of the problem as described in the statement of task (Box 1-1) as well as the approach taken by the committee. Chapter 2 examines the FAA's current and future cybersecurity landscape and challenges. Chapter 3 provides a discussion of human resource and management approaches relative to a diverse and effective FAA cybersecurity workforce, using the employee lifecycle model. Chapter 4 continues using the adapted employee lifecycle model and describes the organizational structure, workforce strategies, best practices, and lessons learned that can be applied to the FAA's cybersecurity workforce. Chapter 5 uses the findings, conclusions, and recommendations presented in the earlier chapters to articulate the key challenges for the FAA and present action items for several key opportunities. Appendix A lists the agendas and speakers from the various data-gathering workshops and open meetings that were held to fulfill the statement of task. The committee member's biographies can be found in Appendix B.

REFERENCES

The Business-Higher Education Forum. 2017. *Invest to Improve: The Cybersecurity Talent Deficit*. Available: https://www.bhef.com/sites/default/files/bhef_2017_invest_to_improve.pdf.

CSIS (Center for Strategic and International Studies). 2016. *Hacking the Skills Shortage: A Study of International Shortage in Cybersecurity Skills*. Available: https://www.mcafee.com/enterprise/en-us/assets/reports/rp-hacking-skills-shortage.pdf.

FAA (Federal Aviation Administration). 2020. "The FAA Cybersecurity Workforce Overview." Presentation to Committee on Cybersecurity Workforce of the Federal Aviation Administration by FAA Cybersecurity Steering Committee (CSC) and FAA AHR Representatives. February 19, 2020. Washington, DC.

Hernandez, S. 2020. *Government Cyber Workforce Challenges*. Presentation to Committee on Cybersecurity Workforce of the Federal Aviation Administration. February 20, 2020. Washington, DC.

Levine, S.S., Apfelbaum, E.P., Bernard, M., Bartelt, V.L., Zajac, E.J., and Stark, D. 2014. Ethnic diversity deflates price bubbles. *Proceedings of the National Academy of Sciences*, 111(52), 18524–18529.

NASEM (National Academies of Sciences, Engineering, and Medicine). 2017. *Foundational Cybersecurity Research: Improving Science, Engineering, and Institutions*. Washington, DC: The National Academies Press. doi: 10.17226/24676.

NIST (National Institute of Standards and Technology). 2017. *National Initiative for Cybersecurity Education (NICE) Cybersecurity Workforce Framework*. NIST Special Publication 800-181. Gaithersburg, MD: NIST. Available: https://nvlpubs.nist.gov/nistpubs/SpecialPublications/NIST.SP.800-181.pdf?trackDocs=NIST.SP.800-181.pdf.

NRC (National Research Council). 2015. *A Review of the Next Generation Air Transportation System: Implications and Importance of System Architecture*. Washington, DC: The National Academies Press. doi: 10.17226/21721.

NRC. 2014. *The Federal Aviation Administration's Approach for Determining Future Air Traffic Controller Staffing Needs*. Washington, DC: The National Academies Press. doi: 10.17226/18824.

NRC. 2013. *Professionalizing the Nation's Cybersecurity Workforce?: Criteria for Decision-Making*. Washington, DC: The National Academies Press. doi: 10.17226/18446.

2

Current and Future Cybersecurity Landscape for the Federal Aviation Administration

This chapter describes the mission and scope of the Federal Aviation Administration (FAA) and the size and diversity of the cybersecurity organization and its employees and provides the context for further discussion.

THE FAA

The FAA Mission

The FAA is an agency housed under the U.S. Department of Transportation (DOT). The continuing mission of the FAA is to ensure the safety and efficiency of civil aviation in the National Airspace System (NAS), its surrounding international waters, and delegated international airspace, and in doing so, to provide the safest, most efficient, aerospace system in the world. The FAA carries out its mission in a variety of ways, including regulation and certification of aircraft, the provision of air traffic control services, continued operational oversight and enforcement, sponsored grants, and applied research and development. It develops, operates, and maintains the air traffic control system for the NAS. The FAA is also responsible for the safe licensing of commercial space transportation launches and re-entries by U.S. entities or from U.S. territories. Additionally, it regulates airport operations and provides grants for airport development.

The FAA derives its primary statutory authority from Title 49. The agency has significant unique flexibilities in both personnel and procurement policies, made possible through legislative relief from various federal government statutory requirements. These flexibilities were first enacted in 1996 and have been modified by subsequent congressional and executive branch actions.

The legislation exempts the FAA from most Title 5 laws and regulations. DOT's Office of Inspector General in 2016 stated:

> FAA has used its personnel reform authorities to change and expand the number of pay systems for its workforce. However, while Congress exempted FAA from most Title 5 laws and regulations, FAA has not leveraged these personnel reform flexibilities. Many of its personnel policies—such as those related to premium pay, leave, and the grievance process—continue to mirror Federal rules. FAA's flexibility has been limited in part by the Agency's unionized workforce, which has negotiated that benefits and other personnel matters be in line with Federal regulations, and other Title 5 requirements that FAA must follow, such as veteran preference. According to a senior FAA Human Resources official, the only difference between FAA's personnel system and the rest of the Federal Government's is compensation. (DOT, 2016, p. 9)

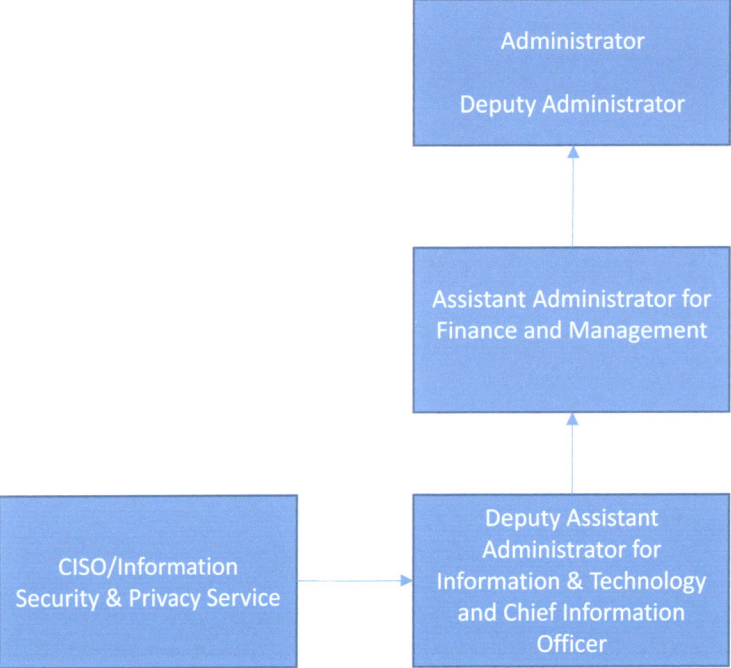

FIGURE 2-1 Federal Aviation Administration Chief Information Security Officer (CISO) reporting structure.

Organization and Structure of the FAA

To carry out its mission, the FAA is organized into five "lines of business" that provide services external to the agency, and nine staff offices that provide the in-house support and expertise for the agency. Each of these 14 units report to the FAA Administrator. The five lines of business are Air Traffic Organization, Aviation Safety, Airports, Commercial Space Transportation, and Security and Hazardous Materials Safety.[1] Like most U.S. government agencies, the staff offices include functions for personnel, legal, policy, and finance. Other services are internally focused. A large staff office is Human Resources Management, which provides agency-wide support for human capital management including employment, compensation and benefits, workplace environment, and learning and development. Specifically relevant to this study, the FAA has implemented a "shared services" staff office to provide agency-wide support for financial management, acquisitions and business services, and information and technology. Thus, the CISO reports to the Chief Information Officer (CIO), who in turn reports to the Assistant Administrator for Finance and Management, who reports to the FAA Administrator. See Figures 2-1 and Figure 2-2.

The largest unit within the FAA that houses cybersecurity professionals is the Air Traffic Organization (ATO). The ATO is responsible for providing safe and efficient air navigation services[2] and consists of air traffic controllers and the personnel who manage the program, and engineers and technical staff responsible for designing, installing, and maintaining the infrastructure needed to perform the functions integral to air traffic control. In addition, the ATO provides technical training for its staff, safety analysis for its operations, and physical and cybersecurity for its assets.

FAA headquarters are in Washington, DC. Additionally, field organizations are located throughout the country and various places in other countries. The FAA William J. Hughes Technical Center, in Atlantic City, New Jersey,

---

[1] More information is available at: https://www.faa.gov/jobs/who_we_are/our_business/#orgchart.
[2] More information is available at: https://www.faa.gov/about/office_org/headquarters_offices/ato/.

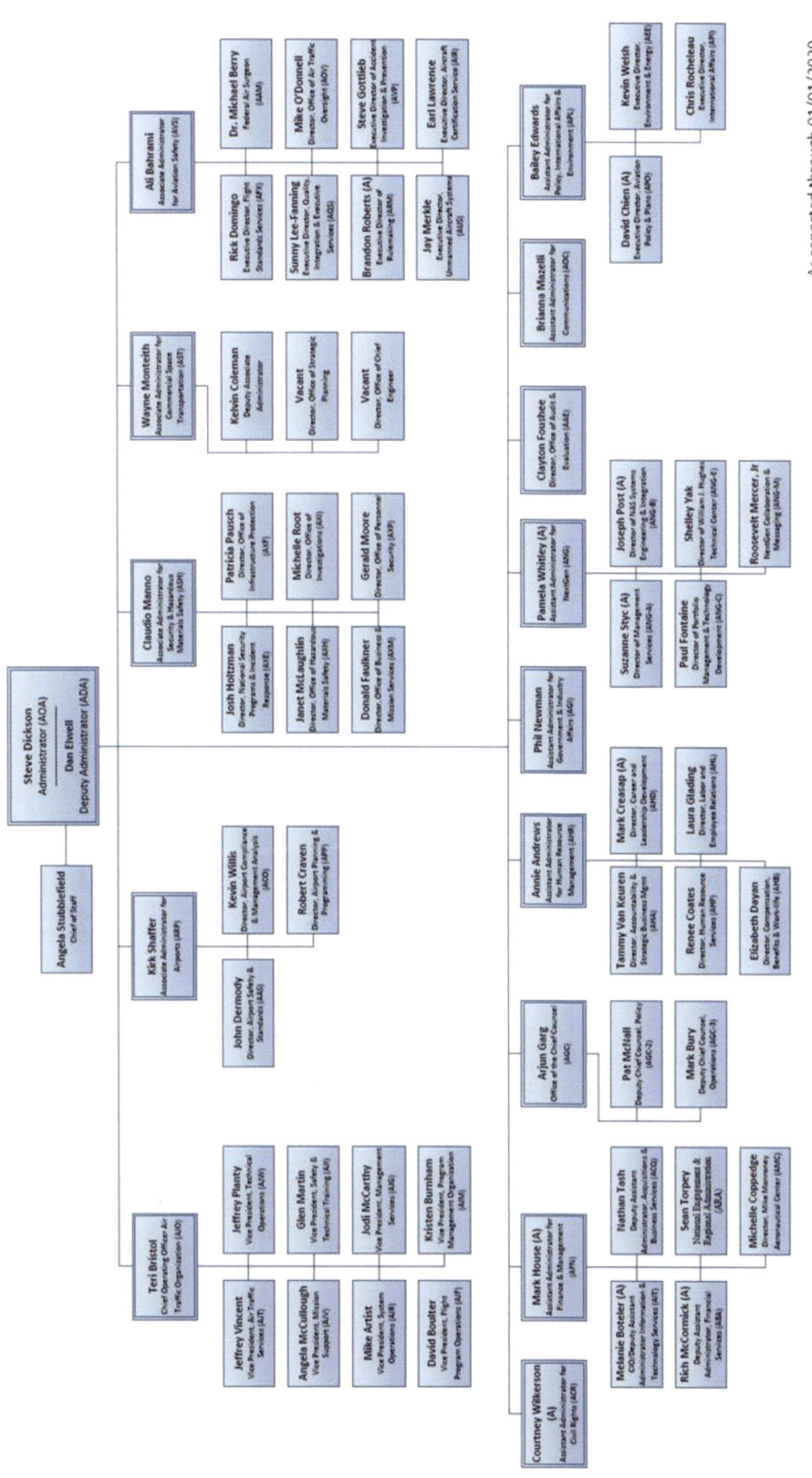

FIGURE 2-2 FAA reporting structure.
SOURCE: FAA, 2020a.

is the nation's premier air transportation laboratory.[3] This center's highly technical workforce conducts testing and evaluation, oversees verification and validation, supports the sustainment of the FAA's full spectrum of aviation systems, and conducts applied research and development. The Mike Monroney Aeronautical Center, located in Oklahoma City, Oklahoma, houses the FAA Academy, the Enterprise Services Center, and several other business support functions.[4]

The FAA's annual budget is approximately $18.1 billion. The operations account, which funds most cybersecurity employees, is approximately $11.0 billion, and is considered, in federal budget parlance, "discretionary" (DOT, 2020, p. 3). This means, as a practical matter, the operations account is subject to annual appropriations and, in the event of a partial government shutdown, is likely to be impacted. In the committee's judgement this has the potential to pose a risk to the cybersecurity program in attracting and retaining cybersecurity professionals.

THE CYBERSECURITY WORKFORCE OF THE FAA

The FAA's Current Cybersecurity Workforce

The total FAA workforce consists of just over 45,000 people[5] located across the globe working in various locations including airports, regional offices and centers, and the Washington, DC, headquarters. There are a wide range of employees including technical, industrial, and business professionals throughout the agency.[6]

Cybersecurity workforce jobs in the FAA, as defined by the National Initiative for Cybersecurity Education (NICE) Cybersecurity Workforce Framework (see Box 2-1) for classifying functions, are not all centralized within the cybersecurity organization, nor are the majority of the employees located at the Washington, DC, headquarters. The FAA's IT and cybersecurity workforce numbers less than 1,400 individuals, who are spread throughout the agency and geographically dispersed across the nation (FAA, 2020b). Just under half of them are organizationally housed in the Office of Information and Technology (AIT). It is common for large public and private organizations to structure in this way—with a central security organization emphasizing professional depth and broad agency perspective, and line experts working on the security priorities of their individual mission teams—using strong informal communication to connect and align actions across the various teams. Nearly 50 percent of the cybersecurity professionals are organizationally housed in the information technology (IT) organization. Of the remaining cybersecurity staff members, approximately 40 percent work for the ATO (FAA, 2020b), and the rest (just over 10%) are engaged with the development of new technology (that is, aligned with agency intelligence and security functions) or in other operational units.

To gain a more robust understanding of its cybersecurity workforce, the FAA analyzed the workforce against the NICE Workforce Framework. Through that process, the FAA identified 53 total roles, including 36 specific cybersecurity roles, 10 general IT (cyber-related) roles, 6 support roles, and 1 "not applicable" role for all others (FAA, 2020a). The major contributing cybersecurity roles that were documented include Cyber Defense Incident Responder, Systems Security Analyst, Security Control Assessor, Security Architect, System Administrators, System Testing and Evaluation Specialist, Systems Security Developer, Cyber Crime Investigator, and Information System Owner (FAA, 2020a).

Geographically, the largest group of cybersecurity employees are based at the William J. Hughes Technical Center in New Jersey, including at least one-half of the ATO cybersecurity employees (FAA, 2020b). The second largest group is based in Oklahoma, including more than one-third of the AIT cybersecurity employees. Washing-

---

[3] More information about the William J. Hughes Technical Center is available at: https://www.faa.gov/about/office_org/headquarters_offices/ang/offices/tc/.

[4] More information about the Mike Monroney Aeronautical Center is available at: https://www.faa.gov/about/office_org/regions_centers/mmac/.

[5] FAA Administrator's Fact Book (December 2020), p. 24. Available at https://www.faa.gov/news/media/2020_Administrators_Fact_Book.pdf.

[6] Data provided by the sponsor to the committee on April, 20, 2020.

> **BOX 2-1**
> **The National Initiative for Cybersecurity Education**
>
> The National Initiative for Cybersecurity Education (NICE), led by the National Institute of Standards and Technology (NIST), is a partnership between the government, academia, and the private sector formed to advance cybersecurity education, training, and workforce development. In 2013, the NICE Cybersecurity Workforce Framework was published by NICE, the Office of the Secretary of Defense, and the Department of Homeland Security (DHS) to offer educators, students, employers, employees, training providers, and policymakers with a logical and reliable method to manage and discuss cybersecurity work, and to serve as a resource to describe and share information about the knowledge, skills, and abilities that will help strengthen an organization's cybersecurity position. It serves to increase communication on identifying, recruiting, developing, and retaining cybersecurity talent. The NICE Framework provides a way of categorizing, organizing, and describing cybersecurity work regardless of where the work occurs. The NICE Framework presents seven different categories of cybersecurity functions (analyze, collect and operate, investigate, operate and maintain, oversee and govern, protect and defend, and securely provision), which are further divided into 33 specialty areas and 52 work roles including the specific knowledge, skills, and abilities required within each role. This can serve as a reference for organizations to further define and provide guidance on cybersecurity education, training, and workforce development.
>
> In November 2020, after feedback from the cybersecurity community, NIST released an updated National Initiative on Cybersecurity Education Workforce Framework for Cybersecurity (NICE Framework; NIST SP-800-181 Rev. 1). In response to the ever-changing nature of cybersecurity work, the authors of the updated framework emphasized "attributes of agility, flexibility, interoperability, and modularity" (Petersen et al., 2020, p. v).[a] The main revisions to the original Framework are structural; for instance, while the initial Framework characterized cybersecurity learners by knowledge, skills, and abilities, the updated Framework has simplified this taxonomy by relying instead on knowledge and skill statements, the latter focusing on a learner's actions. Much like the original Framework, these knowledge and skills match to specific tasks. These tasks, in turn, can define job roles and competencies, enabling organizations to both match learners to specific positions to develop competency-based credentials.[b]
>
> Additional simplifications include removal of previous categories (e.g., securely provision, oversee and govern, protect and defend) and specialty areas (e.g., incident response, threat analysis). These simplifications refocus the Framework around providing basic building blocks of tasks, knowledge, and skills to make a more flexible, modular, and adaptable Framework for organizations (Petersen et al., 2020).
>
> ---
>
> [a]Petersen, R., Santos, D., Smith, M.C., Wetzel, K.A., and Witte, G. 2020. *Workforce Framework for Cybersecurity (NICE Framework)*. SP 800-181 Rev. 1 Supersedes: SP 800-181 (08/07/2017). Gaithersburg, MD: National Institute of Standards and Technology. Available at: https://csrc.nist.gov/publications/detail/sp/800-181/rev-1/final.
> [b]More information is available at: https://www.aspeninstitute.org/programs/cybersecurity-technology-program/ and https://missioncriticalinstitute.org/nice-cybersecurity-workforce-framework/.

ton, DC, headquarters staff, along with staff based in Virginia and Maryland, comprise approximately 20 percent of the workforce (FAA, 2020b).[7]

Nearly one-third of the FAA cybersecurity workforce is female, while women represent only 21 percent of the cybersecurity workforce across North America.[8,9] The committee commends the FAA for this, yet it is important

---

[7]Data confirmed by sponsor on March 29, 2021.

[8]More information about (ISC)² is available at: https://www.isc2.org/-/media/ISC2/Research/2020/Workforce-Study/ISC2ResearchDrivenWhitepaperFINAL.ashx?la=en&hash=2879EE167ACBA7100C330429C7EBC623BAF4E07B.

[9]The 21 percent was based on survey data collected from 3,790 security professionals at all levels, drawn from small, medium, and large organizations throughout North America, Europe, Latin America (LATAM), and the Asia-Pacific region (APAC).

that the FAA does not become complacent and that it continues to focus on developing a diverse workforce. Ethnic diversity in the cybersecurity workforce is similarly imbalanced with combined global minority representation at approximately 26 percent.[10] Within the FAA, more than 66 percent of cybersecurity employees are White (FAA, 2020b). African American or Black employees make up approximately 13 percent of the workforce, Hispanic or Latino employees are approximately 4 percent, and the remaining 17 percent either identified as another ethnic minority or did not specify (FAA, 2020b).[11] The committee encourages the FAA to drill down on the composition of the unknown 17 percent so an accurate accounting of the true minority rate can be made, and appropriate actions can be taken.

Finding 2-1: The FAA can expand representation of both women and minorities in its cybersecurity workforce. The agency is better than average with diversity workforce trends for women but may lag behind global percentages for underrepresented minorities in the cybersecurity workforce. Additional information on the racial composition of the FAA cybersecurity workforce is required to accurately describe the current state.

A growing share of the federal workforce is reaching retirement eligibility, and the FAA is not immune to this reality.[12] The Partnership for Public Service reports that in June 2019, "roughly one-third of employees onboard at the beginning of fiscal 2019 will be eligible to retire by the end of fiscal 2023."[13] For the federal IT workforce, in which most cybersecurity positions are classified, this "age disparity is even more striking . . . , with 19 times more employees over 50 than under 30."[14] Within the FAA, approximately one-fourth of the agency's cybersecurity employees are currently eligible for retirement, and nearly two-thirds of the employees are over age 50 (FAA, 2020b). Anecdotal evidence from the FAA suggests that employees stay past retirement eligibility because they enjoy the mission and are satisfied with the work environment. The seniority-based pay scale can also incentivize longevity. While a workforce with a growing number of workers eligible for retirement can be evidence of strong employee retention, it can also present potential challenges that come with sudden mass retirement and unacceptable levels of organizational knowledge loss.

Finding 2-2: A growing proportion of the cybersecurity workforce of the FAA is reaching retirement eligibility and, as a result, the agency is vulnerable to losing a significant portion of its cybersecurity workforce to retirement.

The FAA is heavily unionized. Managers and employees in certain sensitive positions are excluded from union bargaining units, and while more than 30 percent of the FAA's cybersecurity positions are not represented by a union, nearly 70 percent are (FAA, 2020b). Seventeen different bargaining units in total represent employees identified as holding NICE-defined cybersecurity positions. The largest bargaining unit, under the National Air Traffic Controllers Association umbrella, covers the IT cybersecurity employees and represents 25 percent of the total cybersecurity workforce. Contract staff, who may or may not be represented by a union, also support the agency in cybersecurity functions.

Finding 2-3: Unions represent a significant portion of the FAA cybersecurity workforce and should be considered as integral partners with the FAA in the recruitment and retention of the cybersecurity workforce.

---

[10] More information about the *Innovation Through Inclusion* report is available at: https://www.isc2.org/-/media/Files/Research/Innovation-Through-Inclusion-Report.ashx.

[11] Data confirmed by sponsor on March 29, 2021.

[12] Text modified June 2021 to clarify that the challenges facing the FAA specifically relate to potential near-term labor shortages caused as retirement-eligible employees leave the workforce. Similar changes have been made on the following pages of the report: 23, 38, 59, 61, 66, and 76.

[13] More information is available at: https://ourpublicservice.org/roadmap-for-renewal/talent.

[14] More information is available at: https://ourpublicservice.org/wp-content/uploads/2020/08/A-Time-for-Talent.pdf.

U.S. Cybersecurity Labor Market

It is important to look at the FAA cybersecurity workforce challenges in the context of the U.S. overall labor market. The market for cybersecurity specialists is generally regarded as high demand with insufficient supply. In the cybersecurity field in the United States and world-wide, there is an inadequate supply of cybersecurity professionals to meet the increasing demand (Hernandez, 2020; (ISC)², 2019). The Bureau of Labor Statistics (BLS) predicts employment of the entry-level position of "Information Security Analyst" will grow 31 percent from 2019 to 2029, "much faster than the average for all occupations" (BLS, 2021). Future demand for these positions is projected to be extremely high, and they will be vital to produce inventive solutions to stop hackers from stealing important information or impacting computer networks (BLS, 2021). Median annual pay in 2020 was $103,590[15] for a new candidate with a bachelor's degree and fewer than 5 years of experience. The BLS estimates the total of such jobs in 2019 was 131,000. This includes the private sector, which hires many people from the global labor market. As with other agencies in the federal government, the FAA cybersecurity jobs require U.S. citizenship for security reasons. Because of this requirement, hiring for them can be even more challenging.

Finding 2-4: The FAA's ability to hire cybersecurity workers is further constrained by citizenship and security clearance requirements.

At the higher educational end, the Computing Research Association (CRA) Taulbee Survey reports 77 Cybersecurity Ph.D. graduates last year employed somewhere in North America, of which 5 went into government jobs (Zweben and Bizot, 2019). If the FAA needed someone with cryptographic or advanced systems expertise, it is understandable that competition for candidates would be severe.

This best available data are from before the major economic disruptions of the COVID-19 pandemic and ransomware attacks. Anecdotally, the disruption has led to a number of experienced security professionals laid off from startups, turmoil in the academic supply channel, and rising geopolitical tensions that conceivably could lead to cybersecurity incidents and a spike in demand for staff (CSC, 2020; (ISC)², 2019, 2020). On balance, in the committee's judgment, it will be at least as difficult as in the past to hire Ph.D.-level information security professionals. During the committee's data-gathering sessions the committee heard discussions of the shortage of cybersecurity professionals and how the shortage impacts the hiring of workers (Hernandez, 2020). This will likely intensify the current workforce shortages. An important cautionary note is that the "hiring is hard" theme can mask a hiring process that excludes talented people with nontraditional backgrounds.[16]

Often a cybersecurity job is more than just a job with *cybersecurity* or *security* in the title, so there may be a need for a cybersecurity skill set to be incorporated into many other positions; this need has been identified in the NICE Framework. With the cybersecurity industry changing rapidly, especially in the secure applications development area, careers in the future may also look quite different.

Diversity is one area where a workforce shortage could have serious implications for the FAA. Diversity in thought as well as in cultural backgrounds is an insurance policy against missing vulnerabilities in cybersecurity. It is critical to find authentic, intentional ways to recruit and retain a diverse workforce.

Finding 2-5: The pool of qualified cybersecurity talent is limited, and recruitment challenges will persist.

FAA EMPLOYMENT REGULATIONS

Statutory and Regulatory Requirements

Several pieces of legislation and Office of Management and Budget (OMB) directives have given more prominence to cybersecurity positions. OMB recognized this challenge in 2016 and released OMB Memorandum M-16-15: "Federal Cybersecurity Workforce Strategy," directing agencies to make the cybersecurity workforce

---

[15] More information is available at: https://www.onetonline.org/link/summary/15-1212.00.
[16] More information is available at: http://danluu.com/hiring-lemons/.

a priority (OMB, 2016). The memorandum detailed measures to "identify, expand, recruit, develop, retain, and sustain a capable and competent workforce in key functional areas to address complex and ever-evolving cyber threats" (OMB, 2016, p. 2). In addition, new approaches to tackle constant workforce challenges within the federal government were presented. The OMB projected that there would be a "return on its investment through enhancements to Federal cybersecurity and the improved knowledge, skills, and abilities incoming cybersecurity talent bring to the Federal workforce" (OMB, 2016, p. 2).

In terms of legislation, the Federal Cybersecurity Workforce Assessment Act of 2015 (P.L. 114-113) requires all federal agencies, including the FAA, to undertake several workforce planning activities for the cybersecurity workforce.[17] In particular, the Act requires the U.S. Office of Personnel Management (OPM), in coordination with the National Institute of Standards and Technology (NIST), to develop a cybersecurity coding structure aligning with the work roles identified in the NICE Framework. The Act requires agencies to identify and code all federal IT, cybersecurity, and cyber-related positions. Additionally, agencies must identify cybersecurity work roles of critical need in the workforce.

To meet the requirement, in fiscal 2019, the FAA identified all federal cybersecurity and cyber-related positions and personnel within the agency. The positions and personnel were then categorized based on OPM cybersecurity codes/roles (occupations) for the entire agency.

Institutional Policies

The FAA developed a 2020–2025 Cybersecurity Strategy, which articulates the FAA's five cybersecurity goals (FAA, 2020a).[18] Goal number four relates to building and maintaining workforce capabilities for cybersecurity and lays out four objectives:

- Objective 1: Enhance FAA-wide cybersecurity training, education, and awareness program.
- Objective 2: Support cyber workforce training through participation in exercises.
- Objective 3: Ensure personnel having cybersecurity responsibilities receive appropriate role-based training.
- Objective 4: Enhance FAA competitiveness in cybersecurity hiring and retention through the adoption of the current Federal IT Job Series.

During the first committee data-gathering meeting, the FAA sponsor demonstrated that they have been working to assign the cybersecurity workers to key areas and to ensure that those workers receive the training that is needed to perform their work. In addition, by using the NICE Framework, the FAA has been able to post positions that are more in line with other government agencies' cybersecurity postings (FAA, 2020a).

The GS-334 series was established in 1980 by OPM for the Computer Specialist Series, which was universal across the government. It was replaced with the GS-2210 Information Technology Management Series.[19] However, until 2019, the FAA continued using the 334 series; this meant that if an individual were looking for a job and searching for the 2210 series, they would not necessarily find FAA positions of the 334 series classification. This has now been remedied at the FAA (FAA, 2020a).

Hiring

Numerous cybersecurity workforce challenges are facing the FAA as described throughout this report. Hiring and retaining employees with the right skill sets is one of these challenges. Compared to other federal agencies, the FAA has in the committee's judgement a lower profile among cybersecurity students but has an especially

---

[17] The Federal Cybersecurity Workforce Assessment Act is contained in the Consolidated Appropriations Act of 2016 (Public Law 114-113) enacted on December 18, 2015 (see pgs. 735–737) and available at: https://www.congress.gov/114/plaws/publ113/PLAW-114publ113.pdf.

[18] Note this strategy document is updated yearly and the title years change. At press the current version is 2021–2026.

[19] More information is available at: https://www.opm.gov/policy-data-oversight/classification-qualifications/general-schedule-qualification-standards/0300/gs-2210-information-technology-management-series/.

appealing mission. Anecdotally, it pays well compared to many competing agencies. Compared to private employers, the FAA may not pay as highly but offers more stable employment and an attractive culture. With regard to the hiring process, identifying, recruiting, and training for the necessary skills is vital. In addition to advertised job requirements, there are additional success factors the committee believes many managers are seeking (e.g., federal government standards of conduct such as trustworthiness and integrity, a team player, mission-driven, go the extra mile). These are qualities the committee believes the FAA strives for because the goal is not only to protect infrastructure, but also to protect safety.

The FAA uses several recruitment and outreach programs to attract recent graduates to a range of STEM roles, including cybersecurity positions, within the agency.[20] There has been significant outreach toward minority-serving institutions, though more could be done. These programs are not "cyber" specific, but rather address general human resources programs employed at the agency.

The FAA recruiting and compensation processes have limitations based in law and regulation. While the FAA has significant unique flexibilities because of legislative relief enacted 25 years ago (OPM, 2018), it has proven difficult in practice to fully exploit these advantages. Subsequent government-wide legislation and executive branch personnel initiatives have amended the FAA's original authority, and there is not always clarity about the application of these initiatives to the FAA. The FAA may also voluntarily adopt some of these government-wide initiatives. The FAA remains part of DOT and the federal government, and agency actions need to be taken within the civilian executive branch context. Thus, DOT, OMB, and OPM may need to be consulted or required to approve processes or procedures. While the FAA has unique personnel authorities, DOT and OMB will often strive for consistency across the department or the government. Therefore, since they can effectively overrule the FAA, this need for consultation or approval can have the effect of limiting the flexibility that appears to exist on paper. In addition, the FAA is heavily unionized, and changes in practices may require bargaining for contract amendments or an impact and implementation agreement.

DOT policies require that most hiring requirements be approved at the department level prior to advertisement and filling, and approval is not guaranteed. Hiring is necessarily impacted by the annual appropriations process, for example. Once approved for filling a position, the FAA has an 80-day hiring model and generally, positions are not open for long periods, but some positions are not filled within 80 days (Audet, 2020).

It can be a lengthy process to onboard a new employee, taking anywhere from 2 months to 1 year, including the initial approval time (Audet, 2020). From a hiring standpoint, by the time an applicant receives a job offer, they have often accepted a position elsewhere. Some of this has to do with the background check process, and some of this has to do with HR processing. For certain jobs, national security clearance is also needed, and that can add an often indeterminant delay.

The President's Management Agenda (PMA) placed an "emphasis on implementing a variety of improved workforce strategies, including . . . maximizing the use of currently available tools and authorities to help address some of [the] most pressing hiring needs."[21] In 2018, OPM authorized new direct-hire appointing authorities for cybersecurity and related positions where a "severe shortage of candidates and/or critical hiring needs" have been identified (OPM, 2018). Even with direct-hire authority for a position, there are parameters specific to the job, and these parameters are often customized further by location.

According to OPM, direct-hire authority is available for use to fill vacant positions (OPM, 2018). Hiring categories are positions that have a severe Shortage of Candidates and/or Critical Hiring Need, which include certain Scientific, Technical, Engineering, and Mathematics (STEM), Cybersecurity, and Specialized Occupations (e.g., Medical Officer).[22] The cybersecurity positions this currently applies to include:

---

[20]Focus group discussion with FAA managers and committee members, August 21, 2020. All discussions were conducted in confidentiality, and the names of the participants are withheld by mutual agreement.

[21]More information is available at: https://www.chcoc.gov/content/delegation-direct-hire-appointing-authority-it-positions.

[22]More information is available at: https://www.opm.gov/policy-data-oversight/hiring-information/direct-hire-authority/#url=Governmentwide-Authority.

- 0800 series Engineer (Cybersecurity-related);[23]
- 0854 series Computer Engineer (Cybersecurity);
- 0855 series Electronics Engineer (Cybersecurity);
- 1550 series Computer Scientist (Cybersecurity); and
- 2210 series Information Technology (IT) Cybersecurity Specialist.

Special appointing authorities[24] may also be used to hire individuals who meet eligibility requirements, which includes authority for:

- Veterans' Recruitment Appointment;
- Thirty Percent or More Disabled Veterans;
- Permanent Noncompetitive Appointments for Spouses of Certain Members of the Armed Forces;
- Recruitment and Appointment of Persons with Disabilities, Severe Physical Disabilities, Psychiatric Disabilities, and Intellectual Disabilities; and
- Returned Peace Corps Volunteers/Present and Former Peace Corps Employees/AmeriCorps Volunteers in Service to America.

Use of direct hiring may be for external permanent, temporary, or time-limited appointments when it is determined there is a severe shortage of candidates, when there is a critical hiring need for a position (or group of positions), or when an individual meets the requirements under special appointing authority. It may not be used if a centralized pool of qualified applicants exists (e.g., Air Traffic Control Specialist, Electronics Technician, and Aviation Safety Inspector), unless it is first coordinated with the Aviation Careers Branch.

Where a union contract is in place, there may be additional requirements or constraints. Generally, union contracts favor seniority over external, but potentially highly qualified, candidates.[25] Open processes ensuring broad opportunities to compete may be more important than speed or exact fit when filling specialized positions. There may also be contractual stipulations that negate the use of specialized recruitment incentives. For example, if a contract specifies an amount of vacation accrual based on seniority, additional vacation time cannot be given to new hires as an inducement to come on board to a bargaining unit position without union agreement.

The FAA participates in DOT-wide internship programs. It also supports its own initiatives, including a Minority-Serving Institutions Internship Program.[26] These programs are not specific to the cybersecurity workforce but could be used by agency management to target institutions with known cybersecurity programs.

Employees often have to be located in a very controlled environment because of the mission; thus for many FAA workers, there are commuting issues and a high cost of living, especially in areas such as Washington, DC. For these areas, there are government-wide locality pay adjustments, with no flexibility at the agency level to pay higher salaries due to location.

Finding 2-6: The FAA is currently under-utilizing flexibilities in personnel management and hiring authority, such as direct-hire authority.

Finding 2-7: The FAA's personnel management practices reward seniority over other forms of performance.

---

[23] More information is available at: https://www.opm.gov/policy-data-oversight/classification-qualifications/general-schedule-qualification-standards/0800/computer-engineering-series-0854/.

[24] More information is available at: https://www.faa.gov/jobs/search_jobs/direct_hiring_authorities/.

[25] More information is available at: https://www.jstor.org/stable/40861921?seq=1#metadata_info_tab_contents and https://smallbusiness.chron.com/seniority-important-union-13338.html.

[26] More information is available at: https://www.faa.gov/jobs/students/internships/minority/.

Retention

Employees looking for career growth, upward promotion, and challenging assignments, may be hard to retain at the FAA.[27] FAA managers have noted issues that are common to other parts of the workforce as well:

- Increasing numbers of employees who are not focused on the FAA's mission;
- Many employees who do not want shift work; and
- Duration a worker can remain in an operational environment that can be intense and where stress is often a factor.

To have a skilled and effective cybersecurity workforce, there is a need to maintain employees' skills and keep them sharp through training as part of retention. The cybersecurity workforce is dealing with an active threat that constantly evolves, so a defensive workforce that is trained and knowledgeable is required, which translates to allocating funding exclusively to training. Employees noted that very specific, very technical training (e.g., for specific software tools) is available, but they believe there would be additional benefit to both the agency and themselves from more exposure to the wider cybersecurity community issues (such as attending conferences) and from general leadership and management skills development.[28]

The FAA has ongoing programs to develop leadership talent from within its workforce. The Program for Emerging Leaders (PEL) and the Senior Leadership Development Program (SLDP) are agency-wide programs for enhancing employees' ability to move into supervisory (PEL) or executive (SLDP) positions.[29] For each of these programs, the employee self-nominates, secures the endorsement of their supervisor and organization, and is selected by an agency panel. In the committee's judgement, these programs have a good overall track record for developing employees, but no data were provided about their specific use in the cybersecurity field.

Exit, attrition, and/or retention data can be used to help with understanding current challenges keeping FAA cybersecurity workers. According to the FAA, the exit survey is optional. It was reported that at best 20 percent take the survey, and the data from the surveys has not been analyzed.[30] The exit-survey process is currently under evaluation, and the expectation is that a completely new process should be in place shortly. It was also noted that attrition reporting parameters were examined and a conclusion was drawn that there was no effective way to do attrition analysis on the "cybersecurity" workforce since it includes many lines of business, in many different position series, performing distinct duties and responsibilities. These individual positions and employees could not be traced to a point where reliable attrition reporting and analysis could be conducted.[31] In the committee's judgement, the information gathered via exit surveys or interviews will be immensely valuable to the organization going forward; such information might lead to changing a specific program/project, cultivating enterprise-wide culture, and/or developing a more robust picture of what new positions might be needed in the future.

The FAA's 2019 Federal Employee Viewpoint Survey results for the agency as a whole were shared with the committee (OPM, 2019). Notable results on the positive side include a sense of the importance of the mission of the FAA, and a willingness to work hard to get the job done. Negative responses included several factors noting that meaningful differences in performance were not recognized or dealt with (OPM, 2019). Because of the size and diversity of the different subunits within the FAA, it is difficult to use these results to draw concrete conclusions about the FAA's cybersecurity workforce, but these sentiments generally coincide with what the committee heard from employee focus groups and sponsor delegates.

Employee and supervisor focus groups were conducted by the committee, with questions posed about challenges on the job, training, and reasons for joining and leaving the FAA. Generally, there was an appreciation for the importance of the FAA's mission, the training opportunities the FAA provides, and the security of a govern-

---

[27] Focus group discussion with FAA employees and committee members, August 20, 2020. All discussions were conducted in confidentiality, and the names of the participants were withheld by mutual agreement.
[28] Focus group discussion with FAA employees and committee members, August 20, 2020.
[29] More information about the program is available at: https://www.faa.gov/jobs/working_here/career_growth_development/.
[30] Sponsor response to committee question. April 20, 2020.
[31] Sponsor response to committee question. April 20, 2020.

ment job. It was noted that there are instances where the FAA pay grades are above the rest of government for similar jobs, and that this was an effective recruiting inducement. Interviewees expressed a desire to interact with the larger cybersecurity community and with the intelligence community. Loss of higher-level security clearances upon moving into cybersecurity was noted as a negative. Many of the participants in the focus groups had been government contractors before joining the FAA. There was appreciation for the work of contractors in the more routine jobs, but some feeling that more interesting and strategic roles were also done by contractors, to the detriment of the FAA and employee opportunity.[32]

Contractors

Competition for providing commercial services and goods to the federal government has increased and decreased over the years and is intended to create savings and efficiency in government functions. Many services that used to be performed within the FAA are now outsourced to contractors who help fill some of the gaps in the existing federal workforce. There are numerous benefits to the federal government in hiring contractors to perform various cybersecurity tasks (FAA, 2020a). For example, contractors can be used without having to invest in the costs of their development. There are also benefits on the employee side. Contractor positions typically pay more, and such positions are easier to apply for and obtain.[33] On the other hand, government positions are known for employment security and stability, better sick and annual leave, and providing a sense of service to the nation. Yet, there are also government workers who can leave their current position and come back the next day as a contractor making more money, while not having to report to their previous supervisors (Hernandez, 2020).

The FAA's Future Cybersecurity Workforce

As result of the FAA expansion of missions and the sophistication of emerging cybersecurity threats, the future FAA cybersecurity workforce will need to adapt by expanding staff skill sets from multiple domains.[34] The cybersecurity workforce will need to continue supporting traditional enterprise infrastructure and security operation center needs, in addition to providing subject matter expertise and program oversight of cybersecurity integration into all aspects of the FAA's missions, including aviation, aerospace management, and unmanned systems. Future needs of the FAA will require a workforce with a broad range of skills to develop and apply policy, governance, and guidance. This is in addition to delivering security engineering acquisition oversight and leading systems testing and evaluation, verification, and validation.

A major technology change is under way in the networking of the NAS. Traditional private-wire services by network providers are becoming unavailable and being replaced by internet protocol (IP) connectivity. Though to some extent one can try to retain the old security architecture using virtual private networking (VPN), the trend in the computing world is toward zero trust security modeling (NSA, 2021; Rose et al., 2020). In this approach, traditional perimeter techniques such as firewalls between the internet and the intranet are written off as unreliable means of defense, even if worth retaining for whatever they can do to slow down attackers. Instead, security comes in the form of restricting data and system access based on strong authentication and authorization of people, endpoint devices, and software versions.

Authentication mechanisms are central to the zero trust security model, and because aviation is an international activity, these are best defined under International Civil Aviation Organization (ICAO) auspices. To implement an international zero trust security model, the International Aviation Trust Framework (IATF) has been established (see section 2.7.2 of Unmanned Aircraft System (UAS) Traffic Management (UTM) Concept of Operations (FAA, 2020c)).

Data integrity is essential to the mission of the NAS. It is hoped that cloud computing, big data analytics, and artificial intelligence will each contribute to better cybersecurity. Solid security hygiene of tested backup,

---

[32] Focus group discussion with FAA employees and committee members, August 20, 2020. Focus group discussion with FAA managers and committee members, August 21, 2020.

[33] More information is available at: https://www.cxcglobal.com/weighing-benefits-drawbacks-contracting.

[34] More information on HHS emerging cybersecurity threats is available at: https://www.nist.gov/system/files/documents/2017/07/28/hhhs_response_to_eo_13800_wfd_rfi_07272017 final.pdf.

cryptographic checksums, least privilege access control, and data provenance tracking provide a foundation for maintaining data integrity. There are also differing data security approaches in traditional aviation safety versus novel UTM operations that will need to be bridged as drones enter controlled airspace.

It should be noted that dramatic changes in the FAA cyber landscape would likely occur in the wake of an attack on National Security Agency systems by skilled adversaries. In the committee's judgement, and if the experience of other organizations is any guide, this sort of attack would drive large changes in cybersecurity workforce and practices. While important, such an event and the consequent changes are outside the scope of this report.

Finding 2-8: Modernization of the NAS relies on increasingly digitized and connected infrastructure. This increases the attack surface for the NAS and poses new cybersecurity threats to aircraft and other connected systems.

SUMMARY

The FAA has made advances to improve its cybersecurity workforce by following the NICE Framework to utilize similar positions as other agencies. The organization still has to make strides in various areas of recruitment and retention to diversify the cybersecurity workforce while having a workforce with a low turnover. Some of this can be done with improved use of internships and direct hire authority, as described in Chapter 3.

Conclusions and Recommendations

With a growing reliance on digital communications, the cyber landscape of the FAA is continuously evolving in order to safeguard its critical function of ensuring safe air travel. Accordingly, the future FAA cybersecurity workforce will need to adapt in order to simultaneously support traditional enterprise infrastructure and security operation center needs, as well as provide subject matter expertise and program oversight of cybersecurity integration into all aspects of FAA's missions.

It is important to recognize the cybersecurity labor market is not only tight today—that is, demand far exceeds supply—but highly dynamic and expected to get much tighter in the future. Furthermore, while historically the FAA's high employee retention rate in cybersecurity has helped it maintain the needed workforce capacity and capability, in the event of widespread retirement, the FAA will likely find it very challenging to restore/rebuild its workforce given its current challenges with recruitment.

CONCLUSION 2-1: The cybersecurity labor market is not only tight today, but highly dynamic and expected to get much tighter in the future.

CONCLUSION 2-2: The cyber landscape of the Federal Aviation Administration (FAA) is continuously evolving. Accordingly, the future FAA cybersecurity workforce will need to adapt in order to simultaneously support traditional enterprise infrastructure and security operation center needs, as well as provide subject matter expertise and program oversight of cybersecurity integration into all aspects of FAA's missions.

RECOMMENDATION 2-1: The cybersecurity workforce within the Federal Aviation Administration (FAA) is generally satisfied and dedicated to the agency's mission. The FAA's high employee retention rate in cybersecurity has helped it maintain the needed workforce capacity and capability, but with a growing proportion of the cybersecurity workforce of the FAA reaching retirement eligibility, the agency is vulnerable to losing a significant portion of its cybersecurity workforce to retirement. However, in the event of widespread retirement, the FAA will likely find it very challenging to restore/rebuild its workforce given its current challenges with recruitment. And thus, the FAA should implement cybersecurity workforce planning strategies that will protect the agency against the potential for sudden and mass retirements.

RECOMMENDATION 2-2: Workforce diversity also strengthens the performance of cybersecurity efforts. The Federal Aviation Administration should expand recruitment efforts to include potential hires from different science, technology, engineering, and mathematics backgrounds and careers.

RECOMMENDATION 2-3: The Federal Aviation Administration's (FAA) ability to hire cybersecurity workers is constrained by citizenship and security clearance requirements. Moreover, the FAA is currently under-utilizing flexibilities in personnel management and hiring authority, such as direct-hire authority The FAA should compare and contrast flexibility with other federal programs in terms of hiring, to identify other agency flexibilities and practices that could be incorporated into FAA hiring.

RECOMMENDATION 2-4: The Federal Aviation Administration (FAA) should compare flexibility with other federal programs in terms of hiring, to identify other agency flexibilities and practices that could be incorporated into FAA hiring.

REFERENCES

Audet, A. 2020. "DOT Human Capital Programs." Presentation to Committee on Cybersecurity Workforce of the Federal Aviation Administration. September 16, 2020. Virtual meeting.

BLS (Bureau of Labor Statistics), U.S. Department of Labor. 2021. *Occupational Outlook Handbook, Information Security Analysts*. Available: https://www.bls.gov/ooh/computer-and-information-technology/information-security-analysts.htm.

CSC (Cyberspace Solarium Commission). 2020. *White Paper #1: Cybersecurity Lessons from the Pandemic*. U.S. Cyberspace Solarium Commission, May 2020. Available: https://www.solarium.gov/public-communications/pandemic-white-paper.

DOT (Department of Transportation). 2020. *Budget Estimates Fiscal Year 2021: Federal Aviation Administration*. Available: https://www.transportation.gov/sites/dot.gov/files/2020-02/FY%202021%20FAA%20President%27s%20Budget.pdf.

DOT. 2016. *Office of Inspector General Audit Report: FAA Reforms Have Not Achieved Expected Cost, Efficiency, and Modernization Outcomes*. Report Number AV-2016-015. Washington, DC: U.S. Department of Transportation, Office of the Secretary of Transportation. Available: http://docplayer.net/19555702-Office-of-inspector-general-audit-report.html.

FAA (Federal Aviation Administration). 2020a. "The FAA Cybersecurity Workforce Overview." Presentation to the Committee on Cybersecurity Workforce of the Federal Aviation Administration by FAA Cybersecurity Steering Committee (CSC) and FAA AHR Representatives. February 19, 2020. Washington, DC.

FAA. 2020b. Spreadsheet of employee data provided by the sponsor to the committee for use in the report. Received via email on April 20, 2020.

FAA. 2020c. *2.7.2 of Unmanned Aircraft System (UAS) Traffic Management (UTM:) Concept of Operations*. v2.0. Washington, DC: Federal Aviation Administration. Available: https://www.faa.gov/uas/research_development/traffic_management/media/UTM_ConOps_v2.pdf.

Hernandez. 2020. "Government Cyber Workforce Challenges." Presentation to the Committee on Cybersecurity Workforce of the Federal Aviation Administration. February 20, 2020. Washington, DC.

(ISC)². 2020. *Cybersecurity Professionals Stand Up to a Pandemic—(ISC)² Cybersecurity Workforce Study, 2020*. Available: https://www.isc2.org/-/media/ISC2/Research/2020/Workforce-Study/ISC2ResearchDrivenWhitepaperFINAL.ashx?la=en&hash=2879EE167ACBA7100C330429C7EBC623BAF4E07B.

(ISC)². 2019. *Strategies for Building and Growing Strong Cybersecurity Teams—(ISC)² Cybersecurity Workforce Study, 2019*. Available at https://www.isc2.org/Research/2019-Cybersecurity-Workforce-Study.

NSA (National Security Agency). 2021. *Embracing a Zero Trust Security Model*. Available: https://media.defense.gov/2021/Feb/25/2002588479/-1/-1/0/CSI_EMBRACING_ZT_SECURITY_MODEL_UOO115131-21.PDF.

OMB (Office of Management and Budget). 2016. *OMB M-16-15 Federal Cybersecurity Workforce Strategy*. Available: https://obamawhitehouse.archives.gov/sites/default/files/omb/memoranda/2016/m-16-15.pdf.

OPM (Office of Personnel Management). 2019. *Federal Employee Viewpoint Survey: Department of Transportation Federal Aviation Administration (FAA)*. Washington, DC: Office of Personnel Management.

OPM (Office of Personnel Management). 2018. *Announcing Government-wide Direct Hire Appoint Authorities*. Available: https://chcoc.gov/content/announcing-government-wide-direct-hire-appointing-authorities.

Petersen, R., Santos, D., Smith, M.C., Wetzel, K.A., and Witte, G. 2020. *Workforce Framework for Cybersecurity (NICE Framework)*. SP 800-181 Rev. 1 Supersedes: SP 800-181 (08/07/2017). Gaithersburg, MD: National Institute of Standards and Technology. Available: https://csrc.nist.gov/publications/detail/sp/800-181/rev-1/final.

Rose, S., Borchert, O., Mitchell, S., and Connelly, S. 2020. *Zero Trust Architecture*. NIST SP 800-207. Gaithersburg, MD: National Institute of Standards and Technology.

Zweben, S., and Bizot, B. 2019. *2019 Taulbee Survey: Total Undergrad CS Enrollment Rises Again, but with Fewer New Majors; Doctoral Degree Production Recovers from Last Year's Dip*. Computing Research Association. Available: https://cra.org/wp-content/uploads/2020/05/2019-Taulbee-Survey.pdf.

3

Managing the Career/Employee Lifecycle for a Diverse Cybersecurity Workforce

CHAPTER OVERVIEW

This chapter and the next provide a discussion of human resource and management approaches as they relate to a diverse and effective Federal Aviation Administration (FAA) cybersecurity workforce. The discussion uses the employee lifecycle model (ELC), a widely adopted across industry as a human capital management approach (Burke, ND; Lowenstein, 2017; Santos 2019). This model allows for a holistic understanding of workforce needs and strategies, with each stage offering opportunities to address general workforce needs and also focus on specific considerations related to compensation, diversity, organizational culture and mindsets.

The ELC divides an employee's career into six stages: (1) *attraction*, (2) *recruitment and hiring (onboarding)*, (3) *development,* (4) *advancement*, (5) *retention*, and (6) *retirement (separation)*. Managing an employee's success, and thus the organization's success happens over the entirety of this career cycle. See Box 3-1 for more information on the ELC model.

A diverse, cyber-aware workforce and a security mindset across the organization are essential for effectively maintaining a strong cybersecurity workforce. These characteristics can be best developed and maintained when integrated into the beginning of the human capital process. Figure 3-1 shows the committee's adaptation of the ELC model for this report. The adaptation targets the key items that the committee felt were important to this project. It also incorporates important concepts that an organization should look at in all the phases of the ELC: organizational culture, mindsets, diversity, and compensation.

This chapter and the next use this adapted ELC model to structure the discussion about building a diverse cybersecurity workforce that can support the FAA's needs in the 21st century. The chapter begins with an overview of the current cybersecurity workforce, which serves as a background for the subsequent discussion of specific practices and needs. Following this overview, the chapter elaborates on the first and second stages of the ELC model, "Recruitment and Hiring" and "Development and Advancement." For each of these two stages, the committee begins with a consideration of aspects of these stages as they pertain to cyber organizations in general and then considers implications in light of the FAA's particular needs and capacities. Chapter 4 discusses the third and fourth stages of the ELC model, "Retention" and "Retirement."

BOX 3-1
The Employee Lifecycle Model

The **employee lifecycle** model (ELC) is an organizational method used to visualize how an **employee** engages with the company they are a part of. There are six stages involved in this model: Attraction, Recruitment, Onboarding, Development, Retention, and Separation.

1. Attraction - The first stage of the employee lifecycle is the employee attraction stage. Regardless of how innovative and strong your product or service is, without the attraction and retention of great talent, your company will fail. This makes the attraction stage one of the most crucial aspects to any organization's growth strategy.

2. Recruitment - The second stage of the employee lifecycle is the employee recruitment stage, the period where you seek out and recruit the best talent to join your organization. Recruitment can occur as a result of an existing role becoming vacant or a new position being created altogether. The best types of recruitment plans offer an optimal candidate experience, support collaborative hiring centered around clear criteria and processes, and provide meaningful data that can be used to improve hiring results over time.

3. Onboarding - The next stage of the employee lifecycle model is the employee onboarding stage. Occurring after you have recruited the top talent, the onboarding period is critical to getting your new hires well-adjusted to the organizational environment and performance aspects of their new job as quickly and smoothly as possible. During the onboarding stage, new employees cover more in-depth aspects of their position, and identify the attitudes, knowledge, skills, and behaviors that are required to function effectively within the organization.

4. Development - The following stage of the employee lifecycle model is the employee development stage. It is during this period that you begin to consistently encourage professional development amongst your team, which acts as a catalyst in their skill development and also helps provide them with a future career path within the company.

5. Retention - The fifth stage of the lifecycle model is the employee retention stage. It is here that you focus your energies on keeping your top employees, and ensuring they are happy and sufficiently challenged in their respective roles within the team. The influence of company culture goes a long way in this stage. If the culture in your organization is poor, it inevitably leads to a high employee turnover rate, meaning you will have to face replacement costs regularly. Improving the retention stage is a great way to counteract this risk and promote longevity and satisfaction amongst your team's career paths.

6. Separation - The final stage of the employee lifecycle is the employee separation stage. For most employees, there comes a point where their employment lifecycle will reach its conclusion, whether from retirement, new employment, or for personal reasons. Treating the separation process with equal importance as the onboarding process and being equally as strategic in how you approach this stage is critical. When a team member leaves, it has an effect on other members.

SOURCE: Reproduced from Barr, Emily. 2020. "The 6 Stages of the Employee Life Cycle." *SpriggHR.com*. Available at: https://sprigghr.com/blog/360-degree-continuous-feedback/the-6-stages-of-the-employee-life-cycle/.

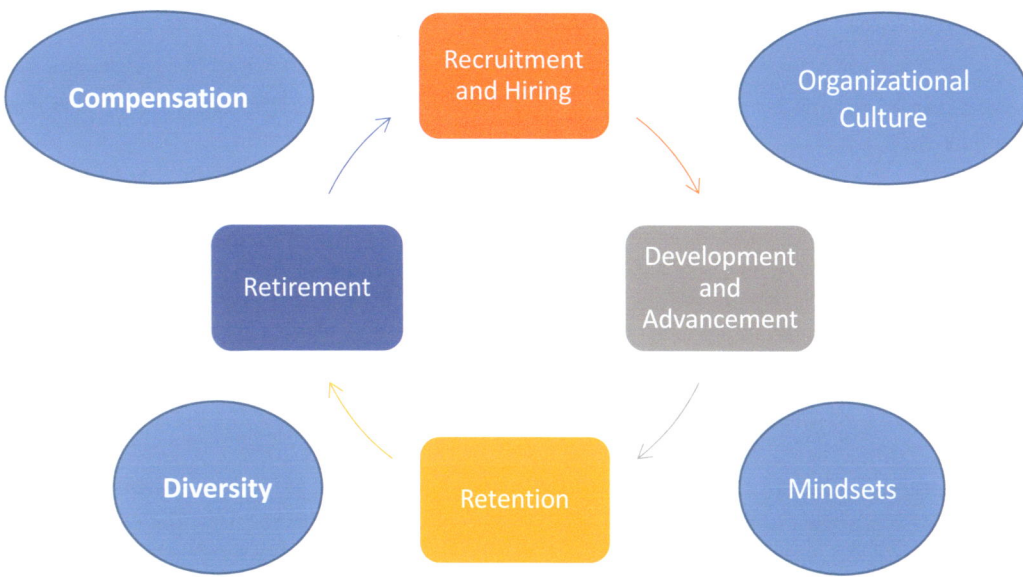

FIGURE 3-1 Committee adaptation of the employee lifecycle (ELC) model.

CHARACTERISTICS OF THE CYBERSECURITY WORKFORCE IN THE 21ST CENTURY

Before investigating specific stages of the ELC as a way of understanding best practices for cyber organizations, it is helpful to have a cursory understanding of the current cybersecurity workforce as a whole. This section discusses three key features of this workforce: characteristics of the cybersecurity workforce, the cybersecurity workforce labor market, and diversity in the 21st century cybersecurity workforce.

Characteristics of the Cybersecurity Workforce

To address the rapidly evolving cybersecurity threat landscape, the cybersecurity workforce requires a variety of skills and the flexibility to quickly adapt to a changing environment. This is in part a function of the dynamic processes involved with adaptation to the attackers who continue to evolve and adapt (NASEM, 2017). The *Cybersecurity Workforce Development Toolkit: How to Build a Strong Cybersecurity Workforce* discusses the characteristics of high-performing cybersecurity teams (DHS, 2016). The toolkit (p. 5) states that a team should be

- Agile: Attacks can emerge at any time; teams must be ready to change course and solve problems quickly.
- Multifunctional: Teams need diverse knowledge and skills to perform many activities.
- Dynamic: To respond to new threats, teams need to always learn new skills and methodologies to secure systems.
- Flexible: Strong teams can shift priorities to meet the challenge of the day.
- Informal: Cyber teams favor flexible work hours and shifting duties to remain engaged and on top of their game.

In addition to considering broad characteristics of the workforce, organizations must also consider the specific operational needs of their cyber operations (NRC, 2013). The National Initiative Cybersecurity Education (NICE) Cybersecurity Workforce Framework (see Box 2-1) helps organizations to identify these needs by outlining job tasks for cyber workers and assigning to these tasks related knowledge and skills to help match learners to the workforce.

Cybersecurity Workforce Labor Market

As stated by Dreibelbis and colleagues (2018, p. 352), "A robust cybersecurity strategy begins with selecting the right people to identify, build, and protect an organization's cyber defense systems. The reality is, however, that finding and selecting the right talent is more challenging than ever." The national need for trained cybersecurity professionals across both industry and government is documented, and globally estimates predict 3.5 million cybersecurity positions will be unfilled by the end of 2021 (Morgan, 2017). According to Cyber Seek, as of April 2021, the United States has a total employed cybersecurity workforce consisting of 941,904 people, and there are currently 521,617 unfilled positions. Cyber Seek, is a project supported by NICE, a program of the National Institute of Standards and Technology (NIST) in the U.S. Department of Commerce.[1] Given the global shortage of cybersecurity professionals, every federal agency will be continuing to compete for a relatively small number of cybersecurity professionals, and therefore a robust long-term strategy for ensuring a cybersecurity workforce will rely on growing the pool of available candidates and developing the required skills in the existing workforce.

The gaps are not only in the number of cybersecurity professionals but also in the skills of the existing professionals to meet job requirements. The estimated global gap of more than 3 million cybersecurity professionals and a recognized skills gap in the available workforce (Oltsik, 2017; Wright, 2015) persists even though there are a prolific number of academic and industry-based training programs for cybersecurity. For example, 59 percent of organizations noted the lack of qualification of job candidates in cybersecurity professions, and once hired, individuals in cybersecurity positions also report a lack of training, which is needed to stay abreast of the most recent vulnerabilities and countermeasures (Oltsik, 2017; Wright, 2015).[2]

Diversity in the 21st Century Cybersecurity Workforce

Diversity is a necessary and integral part of any human resource and management program. The cybersecurity field includes *"the creation, operation, analysis, and testing of secure computer systems"* (JFT, 2017). The breadth of the tasks, coupled with the constantly evolving threat environment, necessitates a workforce with a diverse set of skills, backgrounds, and experiences.

When solving complex problems, having a variety of backgrounds gives a richer foundation for finding solutions. As discussed in Chapter 1, it is important to recruit, select, and train candidates from diverse backgrounds not only because it is the "right thing to do" and a rational response to changing demographics, but also because increasing diversity in the workforce fosters diversity of thought, which is an advantage in cognitively demanding occupations such as those in cybersecurity (Page, 2019; Smith-Doerr et al., 2017). Research consistently demonstrates that teams with diverse perspectives outperform homogeneous teams (Smith-Doerr et al., 2017; Tadmor et al., 2012; Wang et al., 2019). Increasing the pool of diverse candidates through recruitment and workforce development will likely increase the number of qualified candidates and improve decision making.

Diverse perspectives come from diversity in the gender, racial, education, and cultural background of teams. Devon Bryan, the executive vice president and the Chief Information Security Officer (CISO) for the National IT Organization of the Federal Reserve System, and co-founder of the International Consortium of Minority Cyber Security Professionals (ICMCP), discussed the need for diversity in a cybersecurity workforce in a recent interview.[3] He stated:

> No one would disagree that cybersecurity is one of the most critical risks we face from a national economic and a national security perspective . . . And certainly, a woeful lack of participation by large segments of our population in women and people of color, especially when you juxtapose that against the number of unfilled jobs each year and, certainly again, juxtaposed against what we know to be a dramatic rise in cyber crime…

---

[1] More information is available at: https://www.cyberseek.org/heatmap.html.

[2] More information is available at: https://www.isaca.org/go/state-of-cybersecurity-2020.

[3] *The Need for Diversity in a Cyber Security Workforce: Leading High-Performance Cyber Teams as a Recipe for Success.* Interview of Devon Bryan by Andy Bonillo. Article written by Jeff Orr. August 1, 2019. Available at: https://www.cshub.com/interviews/interviews/the-need-for-diversity-in-a-cyber-security-workforce.

High-performing teams typically constitute folks from diverse perspectives, which include diversity of thought, diversity of opinions, and diversity of backgrounds. And certainly, being all in and making sure that all perspectives, all opinions are being brought to bear and with the cybersecurity challenges as real as they are, we certainly have to tackle and approach the problem in a significantly different way than we've done in the past to try and keep abreast of what the bad actors are doing.

To meet this imperative for workforce diversity, employers can leverage programs such as Women in Cybersecurity (WiCyS) and ICMCP, which are designed to increase the participation of women and underrepresented people of color in the cybersecurity workforce.

Diversifying the cybersecurity workforce extends beyond the recruitment stage and is considered below at every stage of the ELC. The mere addition of a small number of employees from underrepresented groups does not significantly improve the representation of diverse perspectives on teams (Jackson and Joshi, 2004; Mannix and Neal, 2005; Mendelberg et al., 2014). Organizations must also take great care to foster inclusive environments that are both representative of the larger population and supportive of the active participation of all team members.

Finding 3-1: The complexity of challenges that cybersecurity professionals address requires a workforce with a diversity of experiences and cognitive approaches, making diversity a functional imperative of cyber operations.

Finding 3-2: The need for diversity represents an opportunity to grow the talent pool.

RECRUITMENT AND HIRING

In the committee's adapted ELC model, the first stage is recruitment and hiring, which addresses how organizations recruit candidates and subsequently hire them into the organization. Recruitment focuses on identifying and attracting the appropriate pool of candidates who match the knowledge, skills, abilities, and other characteristics required for competent job performance. Hiring an employee happens after selection. Selection can be considered the process of matching the characteristics and needs of the organization and those of the individual. After recruitment yields a pool of potential candidates, selection systems are utilized to further identify individuals who will fit within the organization and match the job needs. Once a candidate is selected, they go through a hiring process where an offer is made and terms are negotiated and finally the employee is onboarded. After reviewing key aspects of recruitment and selection, including cyber aptitude assessment, this chapter considers federal approaches to talent development and recruitment, as well as federal recruitment flexibilities.

Key Aspects of Recruitment

Recruitment is the first step in the selection process and is therefore essential in building a cybersecurity workforce. Organizational recruitment[4] practices have evolved steadily over the past decades for a variety of reasons, including legal compliance through increased competitiveness and the availability of a global workforce. Darnold and Rynes (2013) discuss the activities and decisions that comprise organizational recruitment, including administrative procedures, selection standards, vacancy characteristics, sources of talent, and recruiters. Each of these aspects influences the recruitment process, which itself involves a series of sub-processes, including "self-selection processes, time-related processes, information-related processes, interactive processes, post-hire adjustment processes, and individual differences" (p. 59). Thus, when addressing its recruitment strategy, an organization needs to be concerned with many facets of the recruitment process.

Darnold and Rynes (2013) describe how the environment of recruitment has changed and is ever-evolving due to transformations in the global economy, the globalization of work, and job choice. Organizational characteris-

---

[4]More information is available at: https://ecommons.cornell.edu/bitstream/handle/1813/75915/Collins13_Organizational_Recruitment_post_print.pdf?sequence=1.

tics such as image, geographic location, and size are important factors to many potential candidates and must be considered as part of the recruitment process. Organizations such as the FAA, which can offer both remote work and several satellite office locations, may have an advantage in attracting talent.

The committee found that research also points to the importance of an organization's brand image. Brand image building, or essentially increasing the familiarity of an organization, is an essential element in turning a potential applicant into an actual applicant (Collins and Stevens, 2002). Collins and Stevens (2002) demonstrate the importance of organizational branding to candidates. They found that to potential candidates, organizational brand-building is related to the organizational image and ultimately organizational attraction, which in turn influences whether a candidate considers a particular organization.

Finding 3-3: Organizational reputation and positioning is a critical component of recruitment and talent attraction efforts.

An organization uses many tools in the recruitment process. Industry approaches to recruiting talent have an ever-larger online component, often incorporating internal job postings (via the company's internal web site), external job postings (e.g., Monster.com and Indeed), and other social media such as Glassdoor, Facebook, LinkedIn, and Twitter. This ever-increasing push toward online recruitment received an intense increase during the pandemic of 2020/2021, when organizations were pushed to carry out core aspects of business via the internet. This online presence brings its own set of challenges, including managing and tracking candidate information. The Reynolds and Dickter (2017) model depict the process as beginning with casting a wide net via resume parsing and search (e.g., web scraping) to identify potential candidates. Algorithmic screening techniques, such as an email campaign with click-through tracking, can help to build a pool. Information culled from social media can be included as well in developing a suitablility composite score of each potential recruit. Those with higher composite scores are targeted for recruiter contact.

Key Aspects of Selection

Generally speaking, in the committee's judgement, organizations have a set of characteristics defined as needs, values, and goals; similarly, applicants have a set of characteristics defined as capabilities, values, and goals. As stated above, selection can be considered the process of matching these parallel sets of characteristics and needs. The better the match between organization and individual, the better the fit between them. This concept of fit is an essential component of a successful organizational selection and retention process. This section looks at the process of determining fit (including assessment of cognitive and personality traits), applicant screening tools, and the role certifications can play in selection.

There are several types of fit to be considered. One type of fit is the match involving the person and the organization (P-O) (Yang et al., 2008). Here, the focus is on the shared values and goals of the two. A second type of fit is between the person and the job (P-J). The better the knowledge, skills, aptitudes, and other characteristics (e.g., non-cognitive factors such as personality) better match the demands of the job. The relationship between P-O fit and organizational attraction is similar in scale to the relationship between P-J fit and organizational attraction (Kristof-Brown et al., 2005). It appears increasingly important to examine P-O and P-J fit simultaneously (Resick et al., 2007); when it is, P-J fit appears more important than P-O fit. Fit assumes validity for improving satisfaction, teamwork, performance, and other outcomes—but a researcher needs the actual outcome data to test/validate that assumption. Finally, depending on the job, other types of fit may become equally important. For example, if the work is team-based then the fit of the applicant within the team (P-T) is a central tenet of selection.[5]

---

[5] More information is available at: https://www.apa.org/ed/accreditation/about/policies/personnel-selection-procedures.pdf, and the AERA/APA/NCME Standards, which contain professional guidelines relevant to personnel testing, are available at: https://www.testingstandards.net/open-access-files.html.

Determining fit is an important part of the selection process, but it can be challenging. A clear and realistic description of job duties allows applicants to identify potential matches for their knowledge, skills, and abilities, which are often presented in a resume. Although a resume is still seen as essential in many applicant situations, the brief format of the resume often does not do justice to the experience or the quality of the applicant's prior work (Reynolds and Dickter, 2017). Federal hiring imposes very particular requirements including a specific format for applications using the USAJobs, the official website for federal government employment, and that can limit a candidate's ability to show their strengths (and weaknesses) thereby excluding qualified candidates from selection.

The selection process also often involves an assessment of candidates' cognitive abilities and personality traits. These assessments need to be made by tests that are both reliable and valid. General and often specific cognitive abilities are determined by a test such as the Armed Services Vocational Aptitude Battery (ASVAB) in the military or the commercially available Wonderlic contemporary cognitive ability test. Personality constructs are often assessed via the Big 5 personality traits or similar measures in the civilian world, or the Tailored Adaptive Personality Assessment System (TAPAS) used by the military. Many other test types (e.g., assessment centers, physical standards, integrity, job knowledge, work sample, and simulations) can be utilized as well if there is a clear linkage between performance on the test and performance on the job. The link between performance on personality[6] and psychological traits[7] is not always straightforward (Pelt et al., 2017; Tisu et al., 2020). For example, one study found that a sample of skilled hackers had a high need for cognition, but that need for cognition did not predict peer-reported skill within that group (Le Blanc and Freeman, 2016).

Selection also involves gathering information on applicants' backgrounds. Applicant screening tools, including questions targeted at specific jobs, are used to provide standardized methods for obtaining background and qualification information on potential candidates. Questions typically focus on work experience and education, including licensing when appropriate. Automated testing in general often plays a role via the administration of standardized tests with established reliability and validity. Behavioral assessment of candidates comes from online assessment centers and simulations incorporating controlled instant messaging, emails, and video email. These techniques can be either fully automated or supported by artificial intelligence (AI) and/or human participants.

The utilization of game-based assessment for selection and, specifically, assessment of professionals is being explored (e.g., Coovert et al., 2017, 2020; Gestwicki and Strumbaugh 2015). Gestwicki and Strumbaugh (2015) argue that currently more than 21 different games can be applied to selection. Such games assess multiple perspectives of an applicant, model scaffold learning progressions, and can present complex situations faced by cyber professionals, thus presenting an assessment in line with the work demands of those in cyber occupations.

Internal referrals, wherein a current employee vouches for an applicant to a given position, can be a valuable source of applicants, and most organizations have a process for handling these referrals. This source can be advantageous to the organization, since the candidate often has received information that helps them consider their fit within the organization and self-screens on that informal information. Darnold and Rynes (2013) observe that an applicant that is referred by an employee is more likely to be given a job offer. Their research indicates that these candidates are more prepared for screening assessments and perform better on scored selection procedures (Donald and Rynes, 2013). A potential limitation is that internal referrals often introduce new workers who resemble the organization's current demographics and culture, which can make it difficult to diversify the workforce and address diversity goals.

Certifications also play a role in the selection of individuals in many of these occupations. While certifications would seem to be at least a practical way to measure competency in cyber job performance, they are not without their detractors, who observe that in some instances, certifications appear not to be predictive of cyber competency (CISA, 2019). As discussed later in this chapter, certifications for a broad field such as cybersecurity can encompass several skill sets.

---

[6] More information is available at: https://blog.hubspot.com/marketing/personality-indicates-job-performance.

[7] More information is available at: https://www.apa.org/topics/predict-job-performance.

Cyber Aptitude Assessment

Assessing for cyber aptitude as part of the selection process will be important as an organization works to expand its cybersecurity workforce. A 2019 study by Coovert and colleagues offers an evaluation of both cognitive and non-cognitive aptitudes and traits important in cyber occupations. The study identified those tests and assessments utilized to screen individuals on those cognitive aptitudes and traits. However, the study found that while cognitive abilities were well covered by existing tests, tools were as readily available for assessing aptitudes for active learning, deductive reasoning, systems thinking, and the traits analytical thinking, adaptability, and situational awareness. The researchers did identify one such tool: a *face valid*[8] approach for assessment—a serious game, which is emerging as a recruitment tool that has been developed to provide a *construct valid*[9] assessment of these other aptitudes and traits (Coovert et al., 2020).

Cognitive and personality factors, however, do not explain all the variance in the success of a selection system and an individual's later competency on the job. Social influences from family, friends, relatives, and other informal sources are important in not only recruitment and selection, but also any subsequent decision to stay with the organization. As early as 2005, Chapman and colleagues pondered that there is an increasing emphasis on the relationship between social influences on organizational and job choice (Chapman et al., 2005).

Federal Cyber Talent Development

The 2016 Office of Management and Budget Memorandum 16-15 on Federal Cybersecurity Workforce Strategy directed the federal government to "act to expand the cybersecurity workforce to meet the increasing demand for talent" (OMB, 2016, p. 1). This section discusses several federal programs aimed at developing cybersecurity talent, as well as the guidance that helps federal agencies define their cybersecurity workforce. This section further describes the cultivation of talent before hiring as a way of increasing the candidate pool. As such, it differs from development as discussed below in the section on the "Development and Advancement" stage of the ELC model, which focuses on the development of skills and approaches once a person is hired.

Helping to fill these work cyber roles has been the aim of a significant number of federal talent development programs and regulations. In 2000, the CyberCorps® Scholarship for Service Program (SFS) was formed as part of the Federal Cyber Service Training and Education Initiative "to enhance the security of critical information infrastructure, increase the national capacity of educating IT specialists in Information Assurance (IA) disciplines, produce new entrants into the Government IA workforce, increase national Research & Development (R&D) capabilities in IA, and strengthen partnerships between institutions of higher learning and relevant employment sectors."[10] SFS provides grant support for students earning degrees in areas relevant to cybersecurity in exchange for a commitment to work for a federal, state, local, or tribal government agency after graduation. As of January 2020, 4,040 individuals have received SFS scholarships, 2,834 individuals have entered government service in 357 government organizations, and more than 1,000 are still in the academic phase. Of those, about 95 percent have been placed in a federal agency (Piotrowski, 2020). In fall 2019, a survey was sent to 1,164 SFS students that have already completed their public service obligation. Of the 403 individuals who responded to the survey, 65 percent stated that they are still working in the SFS covered position (i.e., beyond the required period). Of the remaining 35 percent of the responders, 23 percent are working in the private sector, 10 percent are working for the government as a contractor, and 2 percent are either self-employed or not working (Piotrowski, 2020). This suggests that opportunities that expose young professionals to government work can help to recruit individuals to a long-term commitment to public service cybersecurity as a career.

---

[8] Face validity refers to selection or other procedures that appear relevant from the candidate's perspective regardless of any empirical evidence of validity (Tippins et al., 2018, pp. 26–27).

[9] Construct validity refers to the assessment of a concept or characteristic of individuals inferred from empirical evidence and theory (Tippins et al., 2018, p. 46).

[10] More information about the history of the Scholarship for Service Program is available at: https://www.sfs.opm.gov/Overview-History.aspx.

The Cybersecurity Enhancement Act of 2014 stated that the director of the National Science Foundation, in coordination with the director of the Office of Personnel Management (OPM) and the Secretary of Homeland Security (DHS),

> shall continue a Federal cyber Scholarship-For-Service program to recruit and train the next generation of information technology professionals, industrial control system security professionals, and security managers to meet the needs of the cybersecurity mission for Federal, State, local, and tribal governments; provide scholarships through qualified institutions of higher education, including community colleges; provide the scholarship recipients with summer internship opportunities; and, prioritize the employment placement of scholarship recipients in the Federal Government.[11]

For younger students, NIST also funded five pilot programs for the Regional Alliances and Multistakeholder Partnerships to Stimulate (RAMPS) Cybersecurity Education and Workforce Development in 2016. The pilot programs worked to address cybersecurity workforce needs in their region through academic partnerships between regional groups of K–12 schools, colleges, and local employers.[12] Analyzing the methods and best practices used by each program led to the creation of a plan developing comparable regional alliances through such partnerships (Santos et al., 2020).

Two years later, the 2018 National Defense Authorization Act (115th Congress Public Law 91) "prioritized the employment placement of at least 80 percent of scholarship recipients in an executive agency" (p. 131). In addition, it directed the development and implementation of a "pilot program at not more than 10, but at least 5, community colleges to provide scholarships to eligible students who (1) are pursuing associate degrees or specialized program certifications in the field of cybersecurity; and, (2) (A) have bachelor's degrees; or (B) are Veterans of the Armed Forces" (p. 475). The Act also provided "awards to improve cybersecurity education at the kindergarten through grade 12 level—(A) to increase interest in cybersecurity careers; (B) to help students practice correct and safe online behavior and understand the foundational principles of cybersecurity; (C) to improve teaching methods for delivering cybersecurity content for kindergarten through grade 12 computer science curricula; and (D) to promote teacher recruitment in the field of cybersecurity" (p. 475).

Recruitment for cyber roles typically targets individuals with an early interest in the field. It has become common for interest camps and competitions to feature cyber activities. These typically occur for individuals as early as junior high and high school, such as the Air Force's Wright Scholars program[13] or the Girls Go CyberStart.[14] During these intense summer programs, students have the opportunity to develop skills and further their interest in cyber activities. Continuing through college, groups such as the National Collegiate Cyber Defense Competition[15] bring together highly skilled individuals about to enter the cyber workforce.

Federal Recruitment

Workforce development strategy for federal employers must also align with the requirements for government hiring. At the broadest level, these requirements are set forth by the OPM for federal civil service agencies such as the FAA. Under the OPM process, agencies must progress through a defined series of steps that include reviewing workforce needs, submitting a Request for Personnel Action (RPA) to OPM for approval, drafting a position description, comparing the knowledge and skills of the drafted position against an organization's strategic needs, posting a job on the official USAJobs website, reviewing candidates, interviewing candidates, and extending a formal offer.

---

[11] The full description is available at: https://www.congress.gov/bill/113th-congress/senate-bill/1353/text.
[12] Program descriptions are available at: https://www.nist.gov/itl/applied-cybersecurity/nice/regional-alliances-and-multistakeholderpartnerships-stimulate-ramps.
[13] More information is available at: https://afrlscholars.usra.edu/locations/wright-patterson/.
[14] More information is available at: https://girlsgocyberstart.org/.
[15] More information is available at: http://www.nationalccdc.org/.

Additionally, OPM rules also mandate certain factors, such as Veteran's preference, when assessing applications for a specific posting. These requirements often lead to a lengthy period between a position being posted and its being filled, though hiring-side tools such as the DHS PushButton PD™ Tool,[16] which allow agencies to easily draft a position description describing an opening, have introduced some efficiencies into the process.

Throughout the process, federal agencies are further constrained in the compensation packages they can offer employees. Salaries are typically set through a pay system, the most common of which is the General Schedule (GS). The GS system sets compensation for positions within predetermined bands, using a base salary and locality adjustments.

Federal Recruitment Flexibilities

Agencies can, with proper authorization, supplement the conventional federal hiring system through certain flexibilities. One example of hiring flexibilities is the "on-the-spot hiring" authority, which authorizes an agency to extend a job offer to candidates for specific positions without a required public posting period. As discussed in Chapter 2, the FAA currently uses direct-hire positions, or on-the-spot hiring, "when it is determined there is a severe shortage of candidates, a critical hiring need for a position (or group of positions)."[17] This hiring option can be a particularly effective tool when recruiting highly sought-after candidates that have in-demand skills and help to diversify the agency's workforce. Federal agencies also have the flexibility to request special pay rates for high-demand positions and offer other incentives such as loan repayment assistance for federally insured student loans.

Finding 3-4: To aid in the recruitment process federal agencies are able "To recruit and retain personnel with the critical skills needed to accomplish their missions, federal agencies can offer incentives, such as recruitment, relocation, and retention incentive payments; student loan repayments; annual leave enhancements; and scholarships" (Marinos, 2017).

Finding 3-5: Flexibility of on-the-spot hiring is an important tool for hiring a diverse workforce and aids in the recruitment of diverse candidate.

Due to the often-lengthy process that is typical for onboarding individuals into government roles—one that often ranges from 2 months to a year—it is important to expedite the process wherever possible, especially since private sector employers are often able to offer more attractive positions to high-demand applicants as compared to their government counterparts (Hernandez, 2020).

While the clearance process takes up much of this time and is often an unavoidable aspect of the delay, as of 2014, programs such as the Federal Information Security Modernization Act (FISMA) allow conditional offers of noncompetitive placement to be given at job fairs to interested parties who are graduates of the Scholarship for Service program (Hernandez, 2020). Evidence for the success of this hiring authority can be found in its use by DHS and the Department of Defense, though it should be noted that this initiative takes an enormous amount of coordination, cooperation, and understanding between the Chief Human Capital Officer and the CISO (Hernandez, 2020).

Concerns with this approach often center on the potential for arbitrary or capricious practices or decisions that ignore equal opportunity employment considerations. Therefore, extra sensitivity to issues of diversity, equity, and inclusion should be given when considering the exercise of these hiring authorities (Hernandez, 2020). Overall, there is an apparent need to signal to applicants that this process can be accelerated as a means of increasing the likelihood of their continued interest in positions within government roles in general and the FAA in particular.

Finding 3-6: Certain procedural flexibilities (e.g., on-the-spot hiring) and compensation flexibilities can be useful tools for filling positions in high-demand job markets.

---

[16]More information is available at: https://niccs.us-cert.gov/workforce-development/dhs-pushbuttonpdtm-tool.

[17]Document on hiring flexibilities provided to committee by the FAA. April 20, 2020.

FAA RECRUITMENT AND HIRING

The FAA cybersecurity workforce requirements span multiple disciplines and skill levels. There are many best practices in industry that the FAA could benefit from; these include strategies for recruiting multidisciplinary cybersecurity teams at the junior, mid, and senior levels through lateral hiring practices, academia partnerships, and cybersecurity-focused partnerships. The role of lateral hiring practices (Amankwah-Amoah, 2015) in industry means that companies will compete to hire the best talent as an effective strategy to both address their own needs *and* to compete against other companies. Industry research indicates that career advancement, inclusion, culture, innovation, and mission alignment are key factors in attrition and job movement.[18] Organizations that highlight the diversity of mission, training, and career opportunities coupled with mentorships have been successful at attracting and retaining employees for hard-to-fill cybersecurity positions (Lewis, 2020).

Academia is an important recruiting source. Many computer science majors, including more than one-half of those with a Ph.D., are hired by industry (NASEM, 2019). The concentration of these majors in industry speaks to the high quality of industry's recruiting techniques. Industry insights in attracting highly skilled cybersecurity staff include education reimbursement, defined career paths including those specified in the NICE Framework, (Lewis, 2020; Perez, 2020, Worden and Romero, 2020), mobility, and continuous internal and external learning programs. These organizations also have strong affinity groups and employee resource groups that recognize diversity and inclusion within the organizations.

It should be recognized that computer science is not the only major relevant to cybersecurity. Previously, the singular focus on computer science as the only relevant major has led to siloed organizations (Jacob et al., 2018). Today, however, it is generally accepted that the discipline of cybersecurity is broader than computer science. In fact, multiple majors contribute to cybersecurity enterprises and are key to the mission of cybersecurity. For example, in preparing military cadets, other technical academic majors include information technology, information systems and security, and mathematics and data science (Mack et al., 2019; Spidalieri and McArdle, 2016).

For a specialized field such as cybersecurity, a variety of educational approaches to develop individuals for jobs in the cyber workforce are useful. This can begin rather early in the formal educational process and continue through secondary school, postsecondary programs, college, and beyond. Currently, there are several formal programs that can demonstrate an indication of success for future cyber occupations.

The National Academies' 2018 report *Assessing and Responding to the Computer Science Undergraduate Enrollments* points to some ways to build/foster effective partnerships between academia and industry. For example, partnerships between K–12 curriculum specialists are also important to support early and persistent cybersecurity education to expand pathways to cybersecurity professions. Additionally, the report discussed recommendations on the practice of hiring non-degree holders and preparing them for cybersecurity roles. Finally, the report recognized that scalability in individual performance is critical (NASEM, 2018).

For corporations, engagement with institutions of higher education (e.g., universities, 4-year colleges, and community colleges) provides opportunities for branding, research partnerships, and, ultimately, influencing student preferences such that they seek internships and careers in these corporations. Students can develop affinities for corporations who have integrated their efforts across the university through effective partnership strategies. Sponsoring events on campus, such as hack-a-thons, cybersecurity days, digital badges, and seminars have been effective recruiting tools for corporations. In the committee's judgment, participating in career fairs, alone, does not garner the trust and preferences of students.

Programs such as SFS, discussed above and below, have proven to be an especially effective mechanism to recruit cybersecurity talent into the federal government. Students who participate in the program actively choose to pursue careers in public service and government agencies aggressively compete for the limited number of graduates each year. Agencies with long history of participation in the SFS program, such as the National Security Agency (NSA), have developed strong relationships with many of the universities participating in the SFS program (Cook, 2020). These relationships effectively engage students in the agency mission, culture, and work requirements, and encourage a steady stream of interns and permanent employees.

---

[18] More information is available at: https://cultureplusconsulting.com/2018/10/16/meaning-metrics-for-diversity-and-inclusion/.

Loyalty to organizations may be fostered through full fellowships, scholarships, and student loan forgiveness. The SFS program provides grants to universities to fund scholarships for students pursuing cybersecurity-related degree programs. These scholarships, along with specialized programming offered by host institutions and opportunities for government internships, strengthen student understanding of the importance and prestige of protecting national security through public service cybersecurity careers. The FAA should consider both expanding its participation in the SFS program and developing stand-alone programs that provide student scholarships and opportunities to engage with students via internships and other experiential learning opportunities. Creating a specialized SFS program for the FAA may not be necessary, but reviewing best practices of other federal agencies in securing cybersecurity talent will be important.

Immersive experiences in cybersecurity do not have to take on the traditional design of summer internships. For example, another useful tool includes cooperative agreements (co-ops), where students work at the agency for one or two semesters, while maintaining enrollment at their respective institutions. The FAA could also take advantage of semester or quarter breaks, using them as mini internships for students. Students are often seeking paid opportunities during these times. For example, semester-structured institutions have "intersessions" between fall semester and spring semester. This time period could be as long as 40 days, providing an opportunity for a student to secure an internship and focus on a cybersecurity project. "May-mesters," the break between end of the spring semester and beginning of summer sessions, could also be considered. The inter-sessions are important because they can allow students to continue their academic matriculation and take advantage of internship opportunities. In this way, students can graduate within 4 years, minimize student debt, and pursue their career in cybersecurity in the FAA.

Finding 3-7: Many individuals presently in the FAA report an early interest in aviation.

Finding 3-8: Other agencies are able to interview and extend initial offers on-the-spot during relevant cybersecurity conferences and university career fairs; the FAA should follow this example.

Job Listings

To get a better perspective on the advertising methods and techniques used by agencies and departments of the federal government, the committee reviewed more than 100 job postings for cybersecurity-related positions from the USAJobs.gov and Indeed.com websites.

The review revealed there to be almost no job vacancies for entry- or lower-level applicants as determined by the GS classification system. Notably, among the few found, none of the job postings was aimed at any applicant lower than GS-7, with little to no attention to language that appeared to indicate enthusiasm or effort in the promotion of the agency or posting. Aside from basic qualifications and mission descriptions, there was little effort to solicit applicants through use of high-impact language. These basic phrases include, but are not limited to, calls for "Motivated and highly qualified candidates," mention of a "Strong team environment," or calls to "Come join this dynamic team using your expertise to make a real impact." One listing that stood out among the entry-level to experienced positions was a GS-7 Step 1 cyber mitigation engineer at the NSA, which made appeals to the applicant's potential interest in "securing our nation's critical infrastructure."

Most spoke of their history and founding accomplishments regardless of GS level and used similar key phrases to attempt to draw the applicant in. However, the higher or more senior the job and/or title, the more likely the listing was to use impactful language. Essentially, the higher the GS level, the more the agency or department lobbied for the applicant. Alternatively, the lower GS-level postings put forth little to no effort to accomplish more than list the vacancies as described above. All of the job postings have similar education requirements (across the GS level), incentives were nonexistent, and offered benefits followed government boilerplate. Many higher-level postings, especially those affiliated with a military branch of the federal government or office, used language that attempted to "inspire" and/or appeal to a potential applicant's "patriotism" and sense of duty to their country. Another higher-level posting touted the applicant's role in developing "technologies and tools" and being "a part of cutting-edge innovations."

Suggestions to address gaps or deficiencies in postings:

- Put forth as much effort (if not more) into **"improving recruiting tactics" for lower-entry-level applicants** as in higher/senior level—including **language that conveys a vested interest in applicants' success** and future achievements.
- **Promote agency/department incentives**, that will pay for continued education; training and certifications; more opportunities for merit/step increases.
- Create an **achievable/realistic career agenda and path** so applicant can see that the agency is thinking about their future goals, aspirations, and growth.
- **Promote growth within "career path" plan** so that applicant can visualize (from the start) the payoff for their hard work, allegiance, and "stick to it" mindset.
- A **list of nonconfidential but exciting projects** that the FAA cybersecurity group is engaged with will help potential applicants have a better understanding of the impact of the position.

In job listings, the FAA would benefit from portraying its public persona as the preeminent organization it is. As discussed above, organizational reputation and branding play a central role in attracting high-quality talent. Recent research continues to demonstrate that organizational reputation is a primary determinant of successful recruitment (Baer et al., 2018; Harris et al., 2020; Lawong et al., 2019).

Taking a haphazard approach to hiring in critical skill occupations is rarely successful. Successful attraction is most likely to occur through targeted recruitment practices, even when using social media to attract passive job seekers (Acikgoz, 2019). Furthermore, Ng and Sears (2017) demonstrate that the targeted approach is highly successful even when attempting to attract high-level individuals based on gender.

Scholarship Opportunities and FAA Recruitment

Several scholarship opportunities offer possibilities for the FAA to increase visibility among young and diverse cyber talent. As discussed in detail above, the National Science Foundation's SFS program, established in 2000, provides up to 3 years of tuition support for students pursuing a postsecondary degree in cybersecurity. In exchange for tuition assistance, a living stipend, and limited professional development support, graduates of the SFS program pledge to serve in the federal government for a period of time equal to the length of their support. The program has proven successful in bringing cybersecurity talent into the federal government. According to a 2019 survey of SFS graduates, 65 percent of respondents indicated continued employment with the federal government beyond the mandatory period of their scholarship (Piotrowski, 2020).

According to figures provided by the sponsor, the FAA has not received any placements of SFS graduates. While the agency is considering more engagement with SFS, participants in the SFS program are responsible for finding their own employment and can chose where they work within the federal government. This suggests that the FAA will need to focus its efforts on increasing awareness of its mission among SFS participants to enable it to compete for SFS graduates.

Another program is the Cybersecurity Talent Initiative of the Partnership for Public Service, which mandates 2 years of service in the federal government.[19] This program works with diversity-oriented groups such as WiCyS to create a pool of cyber talent that better reflects national demographics (Kempinski and Cunningham, 2020). By partnering with the Cybersecurity Talent Initiative, current federal partners such as the Federal Bureau of Investigation and the Department of Homeland Security can simultaneously meet their cybersecurity workforce needs and improve diversity in the workplace (Kempinski and Cunningham, 2020). The FAA should consider deeper partnerships with these programs to achieve the same ends.

Finding 3-9: The FAA has not partnered with the SFS program to effectively recruit cyber talent to the organization.

---

[19]More information is available at https://cybertalentinitiative.org/.

Finding 3-10: The FAA has not partnered with universities to shape cybersecurity programs and curricula.

Finding 3-11: The FAA might consider developing its own programs outside of SFS to provide fellowships and scholarship to students, as well as find ways to integrate them early via internships and other experiential learning opportunities.

Recruiting for Diversity in the FAA Cybersecurity Workforce

In cybersecurity, vulnerabilities arise from complexities associated with a variety of threat actors, strategies, technologies, and geopolitical conflicts. To prevent or confront cyber attacks, multiple perspectives are needed. A monoculture in a cybersecurity organization is not helpful when exploring cybersecurity risks. Blind spots created by "group think" can cause vulnerabilities to be missed or ignored. As discussed in the above section on diversity in the 21st century workplace and also in Chapter 1, diversity in cultural backgrounds yields diversity of thought.[20] Diversity in thought as well as in cultural backgrounds can be an insurance policy against missing vulnerabilities.

Group vulnerability assessments, such as the Flaw Hypothesis methodology and the Delphi method described below, are often employed, especially in larger organizations, to aid in developing a risk management plan for the organization. Both methods stress diversity in experience, in thinking, and in cultural/ethnic background.

As described in depth by Bishop (2004), the Flaw Hypothesis methodology is the system analysis and penetration technique in which the specification and documentation for an information system are analyzed to produce a list of hypothetical flaws (Bishop, 2004). This list is prioritized based on the estimated probability a flaw exists, on the ease of exploiting it, and on the extent of control or compromise it would provide. The prioritized list is used to perform penetration testing of a system, the ultimate investment strategy in cybersecurity mitigations (i.e., policy, administrative processes, technologies, awareness training, continues information assurance process).

The Delphi method is a structured communication technique or method, originally developed as a systematic, interactive, and iterative technique that relies on a panel of experts (Adler and Ziglio, 1996). Delphi is based on the principle that decisions from a structured group of individuals are more accurate than those from unstructured group.

Active and ongoing recruiting is a means to diversifying the workforce. It is not effective to simply participate in career fairs or post a position and hope that diverse candidates see the posting and apply. Employers should actively engage in awareness and recruitment activities year-round to ensure that their organization is visible and trusted to potential candidates. During the committee presentations, we heard from representatives of the Department of Education and United States Coast Guard on how they recruit and the tools they employ to hire a diverse cybersecurity workforce. They acknowledged that they have similar challenges to the FAA in hiring cybersecurity professionals due to salary, benefits, and U.S. citizenship requirements (Embry, 2020; Hernandez, 2020).

Increasing the talent pool available to a cybersecurity workforce may require an emphasis on the recruitment of minorities and women, groups that have traditionally been overlooked (Burrell, 2018). Recognizing barriers reported directly by women and underrepresented minorities is critical to finding authentic, intentional ways to recruit and retain a diverse workforce.

Furthermore, obtaining high-quality, diverse candidates to apply requires active engagement in recruitment where those candidates are being educated and trained. For example, several organizations develop and maintain relationships at historically Black colleges and universities (HBCUs). The FAA could prioritize developing meaningful partnerships with minority-serving institutions, professional societies relevant to cybersecurity, and other groups. In the committee's judgment, relationships and innovative partnerships yield results that are beneficial to an organization with a growing population of retirement-eligible personnel.

Finally, the military Veteran workforce is highly talented and experienced, yet many Veterans find it difficult to obtain their first career job after the military (Turner, 2021). The FAA would benefit by expanding its options such that Veterans of all ranks, officer and enlisted, are actively recruited. In the committee's judgment, there are still challenges with officer corps diversity across all military branches, but enlisted personnel are also highly qualified and should be explored as a source of talent in cybersecurity.

---

[20] More information is available at: https://www.diversitywoman.com/diversity-of-thought/.

Finding 3-12: The committee acknowledges that the FAA has similar challenges as other federal agencies to recruit a diverse cybersecurity workforce.

Finding 3-13: The FAA does not take advantage of programs that other agencies use to recruit cybersecurity professionals.

The FAA has had success recruiting people from military backgrounds, both in terms of mission-driven alignment and drawing from a pool that more accurately reflects the demographics of the overall population.[21] In the committee's judgement, the FAA might benefit from enhanced recruiting of people from mission-driven backgrounds such as military Veterans (individuals often seeking continued mission-driven employment). However, it is important that the agency does not rely too much on the military as a way of *increasing* diversity in the cybersecurity workforce so as to avoid *diminishing* diversity of thought by hiring too many workers from a single source.

DEVELOPMENT AND ADVANCEMENT

The ELC model includes talent development and advancement. This is the next step after an organization has successfully identified, recruited, and hired the employee. Employee development can include training and performance management. Training has been adopted as an approach by which employers can adapt their current workforce to evolving challenges and skill requirements of the job. Traditional approaches to training as well as emergent trends, such as serious games and simulations of varying levels of fidelity, can provide levels of customization for employee needs. Key activities in this stage of the cycle include reskilling and training, educational conferences, certification, performance management, and organizational culture. Finally, the committee explores performance management and strategies to cultivate cyber competencies in the workforce.

Reskilling and Training

Hiring employees with the right skill set and then growing them as the job requirements change is optimal. However, when organizations are unable to recruit the talent needed to meet new needs, reskilling can empower the existing workforce to adapt to new challenges. In a field such as cybersecurity, marked by rapid changes in skill sets and high demand for talent, reskilling is a valuable tool for employers. Reskilling is overall very promising, and opportunities exist to help transition reskilled employees to positions relevant to their training; over time, reskilling should grow beyond technical skills to include managerial and operational skills (Hernandez, 2020). Many organizations have developed retaining and reskilling programs to help manage the scarcity of new talent in a competitive labor market by training existing staff to take on cybersecurity roles. Large companies such as Amazon, AT&T, and JP Morgan and Chase have developed reskilling programs, sometimes in partnership with universities (Weber, 2019). In considering reskilling programs, it should be noted that in the committee's judgement their long-term utility has not yet been established.

Those entering the cybersecurity field require ongoing training and education to learn about new technologies and possible threats and to stay adept. A 2014 survey of cyber workers found that 84 percent of participants disclosed informal education supplementation to be a requirement for job success (Champion et al., 2014). Many participants also reported that individuals who had on-the-job training had higher performance.

Finding 3-14: Reskilling is overall very promising, and opportunities exist to help transition reskilled employees to positions relevant to their training.

Online training systems are changing the delivery landscape for training, with training occurring at nearly any time and location. This allows employees to participate in training regardless of location (at work or non-

---

[21] Focus group discussion with FAA employees and committee members, August 20, 2020. All discussions were conducted in confidentiality, and the names of the participants are withheld by mutual agreement.

work location). The FAA presently has a learning management system it utilizes to deliver training,[22] and this type of training, especially courses targeted at cyber, should be encouraged across all levels of the organization. Online training is often organized into learning roadmaps, and if not already targeted for cybersecurity, it would be most helpful to do so.

Training platforms provide an excellent option for certain types of training, especially in situations where it would be beneficial to employ a digital sandbox for individuals to work with specific devices and realistic models of intrusions and attacks. The advantages of this approach are described by Urias and colleagues (2017). Acosta and colleagues (2017) provide further examples, including an emulation sandbox suitable for small to medium scenarios and a logger for capturing and recording evaluator data. Domínguez and colleagues (2017) also demonstrate the efficacy of using real equipment for the training of control systems in security and critical infrastructure protection. Virtual labs can be created via training environments such as RunLabs (Justice and Vyas, 2017), which allow for the rapid configuration of virtual machines with specific network configurations tailored to adaptable training scenarios and scripts.

Serious games (games used for a purpose other than mere entertainment) are being developed for cybersecurity awareness training (Gestwicki and Strumbaugh, 2015; Huynh et al., 2017). The advantages of serious games are that they can be played in the normal work environment and can be constructed to force the player to engage in the material at a deeper level than that required for rote memorization. Storylines can be developed and constructed to help players understand the cybersecurity problems and the advantages of alternative resolutions. It is essential, however, that the serious game employ models of game-based learning to be successful (Coovert et al., 2017; Katsantonis et al., 2017). A survey of serious games in cybersecurity training can be found in Tioh and colleagues (2017).

Gamification (the application of typical elements of gameplay) has established a foothold in the training of first responders focusing on cybercrime (Coull et al., 2017). According to the authors, the gamification approach for training large numbers of police officers holds promise. Gamification has also been used with traditional hands-on skills, such as using capture the flag to foster cybersecurity skills (Li and Kulkarni, 2016).

Due to the fast pace of changes in technology and the fact that security is largely dependent on the environment and context of the work domain, no single training program can cover all the specific technologies, tools, and threats that a cybersecurity professional needs to master to be effective. Training programs that focus on teaching specific technical skills and tools (Caulkins et al., 2016) can leave the learner unprepared for handling new problems. Extensive research in cybersecurity education (McGettrick et al., 2014; Schneider, 2013) has come to the same conclusion—that how a practitioner thinks about problems, rather than the specific technical skills and knowledge, is the key component in the education of effective cybersecurity professionals. In the committee's judgement, effective training should focus on fundamentals and help develop the necessary problem solving and critical thinking skills needed to adapt to the ever-changing world of cybersecurity. The largest gap in the cybersecurity workforce is professionals who have the technical skills in information security and other skills such as communication, management, and can-do integrated thinking about the systems that they are securing (Crumpler and Lewis, 2019; Vogel, 2016). Technical tools and training have been widely and even freely available for decades; however, some of these other, fundamental aspects of education relating to computer security are still lacking, even within the NICE program (Caulkins et al., 2016).

Educational Conferences

Educational conferences, which often contain practical exercises or competitions, also are good opportunities to contact individuals interested in cyber occupations (e.g., DEF CON, Black Hat). These conferences serve multiple purposes, including the continuing education of professionals, the testing of abilities against new cyber challenges, and social networking and teaming throughout. One example of an organization focused on gender is

---

[22]Focus group discussion with FAA managers and committee members, August 21, 2020. All discussions were conducted in confidentiality, and the names of the participants are withheld by mutual agreement.

WiCyS,[23] which assembles women in cybersecurity from academia, research, and industry to share knowledge, and experience, and take part in networking and mentoring. The WiCyS Conference is held annually, and offers companies a chance to connect with students and candidates. The conference is both a career and graduate school fair with a favorable student to nonstudent ratio and content focused on education, research, outreach, and industry opportunities. It is currently the largest security conference in the nation (Siraj, 2020). WiCyS also includes a Veteran Assistance Program to help female Veterans transition into careers in cybersecurity.

With the demand increasing for cybersecurity professionals, effective cybersecurity education is essential to have a qualified workforce. There are numerous formal and informal education efforts under way including professional certifications, college-level internships and scholarships, high school efforts, and earlier school efforts, all discussed below. Early talent investment starting in elementary school can help develop an interest in the cybersecurity field.

Certification

According to NIST, cybersecurity professionals protect the data, systems, and operations of an organization by providing a variety of security-related tasks (Newhouse et al., 2017). In the realm of federal employment, possession of a relevant educational credential or professional certification has played a large role in defining the profession of cybersecurity (see Box 3-2 for the definition used in this report). Figure 3-2 shows a cybersecurity career pathway for an employee.

The broad range of cybersecurity-relevant certifications reflects the variety of tasks and responsibilities that comprise cybersecurity work. It can be difficult to use certifications as a marker of experience because the field is so broad that certifications can be applicable to all parts of the field. That said, while some common certifications reflect competency in a general set of skills, such as the popular CISSP (Certified Information Systems Security Professional) credential, others are tailored to more specific areas and job tasks. For instance, a PenTest+ certification can be useful in identifying individuals with the necessary skills to perform vulnerability analysis and discovery.

There are numerous cybersecurity degrees and certificates offered by educational institutions as well as skill-based certifications. Credentials are granted by professional organizations, educational institutions, and training agencies, all with a range of levels of requirements. The 2020 Global Knowledge IT Skills and Salary Report publishes data from more than 9,500 survey participants; it found that almost 9 out of 10 IT professionals have at least one certification, with almost 4 out of 10 reporting that they are already pursuing another one.[24]

Cybersecurity certificates are typically associated with training or education courses that have a testing component (NRC, 2013). These certificates are often "good for life;" while their relevance decreases over time, they are an indicator of knowledge at a certain point of time (NRC, 2013, p. 17). Other types of certificates need to be renewed; in these cases, "certification is a formal procedure by an authorized or accredited body" based on factors that predict job success (NRC, 2013, p. 18). These credentials require testing and recertification and can be revoked.

The National Initiative for Cybersecurity Careers and Studies (NICCS) website has a list of "well-known industry certifications." Some are meant to be for those entering the cybersecurity field, while others are for those looking to increase their knowledge of potential career opportunities.[25] These include professional certifications, which offer an opportunity to develop applied knowledge and skills aligned with the needs of various sectors such as industry and government. Some of these certifications include the Global Information Assurance Certification (GIAC) Security Essentials (GSEC). The globally recognized CISSP certification is a cybersecurity credential and confirmation of qualifications that is held by 56 percent of cybersecurity professionals (Nessi, 2020). Studies have found that CISSP is a credential many employers are seeking (Wang and D'Cruze, 2019).

Other certifications target specific tasks to be conducted by cybersecurity specialists to prepare for certain types of threats such as the Certified Ethical Hacker (CEH) and the Certified Expert Penetration Tester (CEPT). Other certifications target areas within which the professional should operate. The HealthCare Information Security

---

[23] Additional information on WiCyS is available at: https://www.wicys.org/.
[24] More information is available at: https://www.globalknowledge.com/us-en/content/salary-report/it-skills-and-salary-report/.
[25] More information is available at: https://niccs.us-cert.gov/about-niccs/featured-stories/cybersecurity-certifications.

> **BOX 3-2**
> **What Is a Cybersecurity Professional?**
>
> Presently, there is no one established process or pathway to follow toward becoming a cybersecurity professional, and the question of exactly what a cybersecurity professional is lacks a definitive answer. Cybersecurity concerns are not new, and organizations have long employed staff to handle computer and network security. However, recognition of cybersecurity as a separate field consisting of numerous sub-specialties has taken time. The National Research Council's 2013 report *Professionalizing the Nation's Cybersecurity Workforce* defines professionalization as "(1) education, training, and other activities that transform a worker into a professional and (2) social processes by which an occupation becomes a profession" (p. 15).
>
> Increasing numbers of individuals consider themselves to be cybersecurity professionals based on their job roles and educational and work experience, and professionalization activities are occurring throughout government agencies and the private sector. Professional computer science, computer engineering, and cybersecurity organizations have developed bodies of knowledge and codes of ethics, and workforce development activities are occurring throughout government agencies. There are numerous 2- and 3-year degrees and cybersecurity specializations available, and certificates and certifications in a range of cybersecurity skills and specializations are now obtainable. Government and private sector employers often require or encourage certification for cybersecurity roles.
>
> SOURCE: NRC, 2013.

FIGURE 3-2 Cybersecurity Career Lifecycle (CSCL).
SOURCE: ISSA. Available at: https://www.issa.org/cybersecurity-career-lifecycle/.

and Privacy Practitioner (HISPP) and the Master Mobile Applications Developer (MMAD) will support the development of expertise in application domains with specialized technology, regulations, standards, and operations applicable to those domains of operation.

Those that administer professional certifications are compelled to keep their own certifications active and updated in a competitive market (Knapp et al., 2017). Continuing education is important for certifications, especially in a field that is quickly changing. Many employers are also looking for these certifications to help evaluate the skills and knowledge of applicants, especially among those that lack cybersecurity expertise themselves. Aside from showing an employer evidence of competence, these "may be useful indicators of interest and commitment to work in a field and provide a useful complement or supplement to academic degrees in establishing knowledge and commitment" (NRC, 2013, p. 18). However, earning these credentials and learning the associated skills often come at a financial and time cost to employees.

Non-credential offering organizations, such as the International Consortium of Minority Cybersecurity Professionals (ICMCP), offer annual conferences, partnerships on employment events, and scholarships.[26] Academic scholarships are provided at multiple degree levels, including graduate degrees. The ICMCP tracks workforce and market characteristics in the cybersecurity sector. The organization provides training and certifications to members. Students and professionals have access to publications and resources to prepare for certification examinations and expand knowledge and credentials.

A goal of certifications is to help ensure that the individual who holds the certificate is competent in the area(s) covered by the certification. For the most part, this tends to be the case, as seen in many of the presentations and discussions the committee heard from corporations, who used certifications as a means to identify employee skill sets. It should be noted, however, that some high-performing security teams in the private sector and the government reject this emphasis on certification, preferring to assess candidates and employees directly on practical knowledge of security topics. These groups even claim to observe a negative correlation between certification and real-world skills.

Finding 3-15: Cybersecurity certifications do not necessarily indicate equal aptitude for the myriad of job tasks that constitute cybersecurity work. Specific certifications may indicate high suitability for specialized roles within the cybersecurity workforce.

Finding 3-16: Employers who cannot provide professional certification training and compensation for certification and professional development will likely struggle to attract talent. This challenge and especially the financial burden may deter interested individuals who might otherwise have pursued the necessary credentials.

Performance Management

Performance management within organizations has evolved from older traditional approaches to performance appraisal (Pulakos et al., 2019). In these older approaches, appraisals typically took place in organizations annually and focused on administrative needs, such as who should receive a raise, be promoted, let go, and so forth. The individual performing the assessment (typically one's boss) judged and evaluated the effectiveness of the individual in meeting job and organizational needs over the year. A second approach (split role) evolved and eventually became widespread; proposed by Meyer, Kay, and French (1981), in this approach, the individual is not only judged, but also receives developmental feedback (Pulakos et al., 2019).

Today, performance management in many organizations is a continuous process, no longer performed once or twice a year, but as often as necessary (e.g., weekly). It focuses on identifying, measuring, and developing individuals' strengths and weaknesses. Performance management covers the administrative and developmental roles and includes four additional purposes: information, documentation, organizational maintenance, and strategy (Smither and London, 2009). A Lithuanian study found that the informational component keeps the employees up to date on the supervisor's, organization's, and when appropriate, the organization's customer's expectations and their

---

[26] More information about ICMCP is available at: https://www.icmcp.org/.

performance relative to those expectations (Martinaityte et al., 2019). The documentation role codifies information used for various purposes (e.g., promotion, termination). Moving up the level of analysis hierarchy, organization maintenance defines and maintains a talent and competency inventory, which often feeds into a workforce planning system. Finally, the strategic component helps upper and top management achieve business objectives and goals.

An effective performance management system can help ensure there are no surprises to individuals in that they are continually informed of their performance and are provided feedback regarding their performance. As with the developmental component in the original split role approach, there is two-way communication between the ratee and the rater (Meyer et al., 1981). The discussion always should be open, honest, and factual, where performance standards are made clear and effectively communicated. This ensures the ongoing feedback focused on job performance is understood and accepted. Without acceptance, it is unlikely deficient behavior will be modified or changed or that exemplary behavior will emerge (Erez and Kanfer, 1983).

Key aspects of a performance management system are that it needs to be valid, reliable, and acceptable (Ilgen and Feldman, 1983; Murphy and Cleveland, 1991; Tippins et al., 2018). When considering validity, measures need to be relevant to the person/job. This relevance is best developed through a job analysis where the job is described as well as the personal characteristics of individuals who are competent in the job (DeNisi and Murphy, 2017). Reliable and valid measures are relevant to the job, as defined through job analysis. Both structured ratings and rater training help ensure two or more supervisors rating the same individual would have the same ratings when rating the same aspects of an incumbent's performance (DeNisi and Pritchard, 2006). Reliable and valid job analysis also allows for specificity in the performance management system. This allows for a process whereby, when an employee is deficient, the deficiency is communicated along with clear and tangible guidance for remediation and improvement.

Built in this way (based on a reliable and valid job analysis), and when standardized (consistent evaluation over time and across individuals), both effective and ineffective behaviors can be identified and employed in the performance management system. Furthermore, levels of performance can be specified. For example, at each of the following levels, typical behaviors are specified for employees in the 40th percentile, 50th percentile, 85th percentile, and 95th percentile.

Beginning with a reliable and valid job analysis also ensures meaningfulness (face valid) to the employee. Each employee can be assured they are being evaluated on only those aspects of the job relevant to their position and within their control. Other factors that help ensure meaningfulness include measuring performance at an appropriate frequency (e.g., bi-weekly/monthly) and communicating to the individual how the results are used in administrative decisions. Individual employees need to also be kept abreast of training completed by evaluators, which helps ensure evaluators are sampling the behavior of those rated at an appropriate rate, and their ratings are reliable and free from errors, contamination, and biases (Inderrieden et al., 1988; Kim and Holzer, 2016). Furthermore, in an effective performance management system, there needs to be a clear and objective approach for appeals for cases where the ratee feels a mistake has been made, and when appropriate, the error is corrected.

It is important that employees are made aware that the performance management system applies to all employees, including supervisors and managers. This ensures the system is thorough as it reaches throughout the organization. Thoroughness is also ensured by building from an effective job analysis in that all major job duties and responsibilities are identified and included in the performance measurement and management system. This helps make certain that the employee receives feedback not only on areas needing improvement but also on areas done well. The sources of feedback should be any relevant individual or group the individual interacts with during their work. These sources include supervisor, peers, and customers (historically referred to as a 360-degree review), as relevant to each individual.

Finally, for a performance management system to be accepted, it needs to be perceived as fair by all those in the organization it impacts. Fairness is often assessed via three different types of organizational justice: procedural, distributive, and interactional (Cropanzano et al., 2007). Each is subjective and deals with perceptions. The focus on interactional justice can be broken down into interpersonal and informational justice (Cropanzano et al., 2007). Informational justice centers on expectations of performance, feedback, and the justification for administrative decisions. Interpersonal justice deals with perceptions of the design of the performance management system itself and the effectiveness of the implementation. Procedural justice is concerned with how ratings are determined and the relationships between ratings and rewards (as well as negative consequences) (Cropanzano et al., 2007). In the case of distributive justice, perceptions of evaluation are assessed relative to the relationship and linkages between ratings and rewards received. It is important to monitor the advancement of diverse employees through the organization. It should be understood that low representation at higher management levels may discourage lower-level candidates from remaining in the organization. Similarly, engagement programs to maintain the interest of new employees may help improve retention rates (e.g., community service, hackathons, etc.)

In summary, today's performance management system is an evolution of early performance appraisal systems. Performance management is concerned with several essential elements, including describing the job effectively (via a job analysis), ensuring criterion relevance without contamination and deficiency in job duties and responsibilities and the associated ratings by relevant sources (supervisor, peers, customers), providing feedback to the employee in an open, clear and objective manner, and doing everything to facilitate positive perceptions of justice relative to the performance management system.

Diversity and Inclusion in Organizational Culture

Maintaining an inclusive workplace culture is important in attracting and retaining a skilled workforce. It is important to understand how an organization is perceived by current and prospective employees and to take steps to improve the workplace culture so prospective employees feel they will be welcome.

One way that some employers try to improve inclusion is through employee resource groups. Employee resource groups are employee-led groups with shared characteristics or experiences that are designed to foster a sense of belonging and inclusion. These groups are formed around diversity attributes such as ethnic minorities, Veterans, employees with disabilities, and those who identify as LGBTQ+. Resource groups serve as an important tool in developing a workplace culture where members of underrepresented groups feel welcome and represented (Welbourne et al., 2017). That said, forming these affinity groups, while effective from a psychosocial and workplace sense of belongingness, are merely one approach to attract and retain diverse employees.

In the committee's judgment, organizations tend to focus more on reporting diversity than integrating and building organizational climates that support diversity and inclusion. An organization requires a process of adaptation and maturity over time to create an effective culture and climate reflective of diversity and inclusion. Where a climate of diversity and inclusion does not exist, a dedication to change is required at all levels of leadership, requiring each to buy into the commitment to foster diversity and inclusion. For instance, Liggans and colleagues (2018) described the importance of leadership for understanding the perceptions and attitudes unique to this diverse group to retain and maximize the benefit of Veterans' in federal jobs. Leadership buy-in is of singular importance in effecting cultural change within the organization.

In the white paper *Innovation Through Inclusion: The Multicultural Cybersecurity Workforce* (Reed and Acosta-Rubio, 2018), the authors discussed the importance of diversity and culture. Their paper argues that while minority professionals comprise a considerable part of the cybersecurity workforce, they are underrepresented in senior leadership positions. As the authors also reiterated, studies of organizations with racially and ethnically diverse leadership teams demonstrate improved company culture, bottom-line revenues, and confidence in security posture. Additionally, they offered several methods to promote and nurture the success of the group, including "mentorship and training programs, executive leadership programs to promote the advancement of the multicultural workforce, and company-wide recognition programs and events" (p. 8). In the committee's judgment, diversity of leadership will improve the FAA's overall cybersecurity performance.

FAA TALENT DEVELOPMENT AND ADVANCEMENT

Reskilling and Training

The FAA should anticipate the need to significantly and continually retool the cybersecurity skills of its workforce given the rapidly changing nature of the challenge—that is, it should not assume that today's cyber knowledge, skills, and aptitudes are a good predictor of what will be needed in the future.

For example, AI and other automation tools are likely to absorb lower-level tasks, which will place a higher premium on higher-level technical skills such as critical thinking and decision-making skills. These AI automation tools might pose additional cybersecurity threats to the very professionals who are trying to assist. Although the FAA already provides a fair amount of internal training (in person and online), internal courses will not be sufficient where it lags other agencies.

Reskilling options in areas that cannot be met through standard, commercially available training range from leveraging conference workshops and similar sources of up-to-date knowledge to more intensive options such as placing staff (exchange program) at other agencies or federally funded research and development centers (FFRDCs) that are further along. An example of such leading-edge cybersecurity practice is the transition toward "zero-trust network" models.

Finding 3-17: The future FAA cyber workforce will need skills and competencies, certifications, credentials, qualifications, career entry points, and career development pathways to achieve and sustain the mission of the FAA.

Workforce Strategies and Best Practices

Like many organizations, the FAA is facing an increasing challenge of managing and expanding the set of skills required in its cybersecurity workforce. Both industry and government recognize the need for a cybersecurity skill taxonomy using specific position descriptions, training requirements and associated career paths. The FAA's adoption of the NIST NICE Framework is a cybersecurity best practice, resulting in an industry-recognized lexicon for the many disciplines in cybersecurity. The Framework divides these specializations into the categories depicted in Figure 3-3.

The multidisciplinary nature of cybersecurity is demonstrated in the above categories and is explicitly called out in the definition of cybersecurity provided by the Association for Computing Machinery (ACM)[27] Joint Task Force on Cybersecurity Education:

> A computing-based discipline involving technology, people, information, and processes to enable assured operations in the context of adversaries. It involves the creation, operation, analysis, and testing of secure computer systems. It is an interdisciplinary course of study, including aspects of law, policy, human factors, ethics, and risk management (JTF, 2017, p. 16).[28]

Since the implementation of this definition, the NICE Framework (Pub 800-181) has been updated to simplify the creation of work roles using specific building blocks. The new method to identify work roles is more flexible and modularized.[29]

Development of Cybersecurity Awareness in Organizations

Taking an organizational view of cybersecurity from the CISO's vantage point, a model should identify the major elements of a cybersecurity program within an organization and the academic disciplines that support each element, emphasizing the multidisciplinary nature of cybersecurity operations. Based on the model, to develop an efficient cybersecurity program, the CISO would begin with a thorough understanding of the goals of the organization seeking protection. This would guide prioritization of cybersecurity investments. Understanding the organization's goals supports policy development (i.e., this information set will warrant rigorous protection; this one will not). Having established priorities, mitigations would be selected to implement cybersecurity policy—(i.e., will technologies be applied or procedures, or some combination to protect this particular data asset).

---

[27] ACM is a nonprofit trade group based around computing technologies. Founded in 1947, the ACM is an international organization of more than 100,000 members and based in New York City.

[28] In 2017 ACM became the first professional organization to publish curricular guidelines for cybersecurity in which this definition is presented. Prior, NIST in collaboration with NSA had been the primary source for curricular guidance for U.S. universities.

[29] More information is available at: https://nvlpubs.nist.gov/nistpubs/SpecialPublications/NIST.SP.800-181r1.pdf.

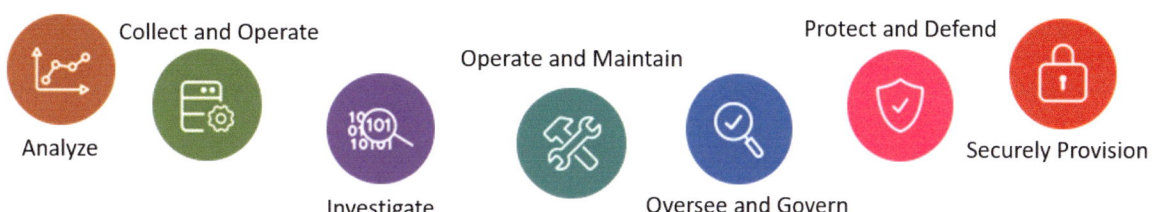

FIGURE 3-3 Specializations of the NICE Framework.
SOURCE: Adapted from https://niccs.cisa.gov/workforce-development/cybersecurity-workforce-framework.

The organization with a digital footprint needs to create a cybersecurity-conscious environment through effective security awareness training so that individuals at all levels have the appropriate knowledge to keep information secure. It takes one individual to deliberately or inadvertently create a vulnerability that could be exploited. Cybersecurity is the responsibility of everyone in the organization.

Finally, cybersecurity is not a static state, but an ever-evolving set of strategies and protocols. Regular (annual or more frequent) audits provide insight into the effectiveness of achieving the goals of the implemented cybersecurity policy. Corrections can be made to reflect audit findings and technology change. As attackers improve their knowledge and skills, defensive cybersecurity must improve and do so using future-oriented and predictive strategies and use an implementation cycle that scales iteratively and toward continuous improvement. The cyber profession also evolves, spawning new specializations that must be understood in order to recruit appropriately.

Academic cybersecurity curricula can be developed for any academic discipline (e.g., business, computer science, information science, library science, and urban planning programs, psychology [resistance to social engineering]), with each curriculum drawing from the same organizational/operational view of cybersecurity and each taking a relevant slice through the model that aligns with its discipline. For example, recognizing that elements ranging from policy to technology keep information secure, curriculum designers might use the model to develop a business curriculum module that would emphasize management aspects of cybersecurity—policy, compliance procedures, developing an organizational culture of security through awareness training.

Coordination with Human Resources

The above view runs counter to the view that many in the general public have that cybersecurity is purely a technical discipline. However, it is not so simple. One of the challenges in closing the talent gap is to provide tools for managers and human resources (HR) to appropriately describe and recruit individuals for required jobs. NICE serves as one of these tools. Beginning with federal agencies, NICE has been used to write job descriptions that effectively communicate requirements to applicants. Creating a common lexicon for describing employment eliminates confusion and wasted effort. Many large employers (e.g., T-Mobile[30]) are now adopting the NICE Framework in their HR processes.

Using the NICE Framework as a Guide to Identify Intense Personal Interest

Using a sports analogue to training cybersecurity experts, an athlete's passion for their chosen sport is accompanied by a desire, almost a craving, to work enthusiastically hard on self-improvement, allowing them to succeed and flourish in their field. The committee members share the opinion of some researchers that a person's commitment to persevere, despite obstacles, and their resilience to overcome setbacks in order to strive for their dreams are a reflection of their internal nature. In other words, intensity to succeed works from the inside out, leveraging passion, and predisposition to a preferred activity and/or outcome.

---

[30] More information is available at: https://www.nist.gov/system/files/documents/2017/08/04/t-mobile.pdf.

In cybersecurity education programs at the Center for Information Assurance and Cybersecurity (CIAC), students are offered a wide array of outside professional activities to assist in finding their passion in cybersecurity. They are encouraged to take multidimensional career assessment tests that measure interests, skills, and work styles to help identify what they like to do and what they are good at. These activities focus students on finding their ideal pathway in cybersecurity using NICE as a guide. In the committee's judgment, when a student is passionate about their choice, they become dedicated to learning—a basis for becoming a lifelong learner that is essential for success in this fast-moving field. Passionate students often join cyber competitions, spend extra time on homework, and seek mentors—all of which accelerates their learning and growth. Application of NICE is useful beyond graduation; graduates may use the NICE Framework to make decisions about their first destination for employment, thus making more informed decisions about the right environment for their own aspirations.

Other tools have been released that may serve as effective career guides. One such tool is the Cyber Career Pathways Tool, which is meant to help individuals identify, build, and navigate a potential cyber career pathway by increasing understanding of the knowledge, skills, and abilities needed to begin, transition, or advance in a cyber career. In the committee's judgment, the Cyber Career Pathways Tool should be shared with individuals looking to start a career in cybersecurity, considering a change within the cyber field, college students, managers, and workforce development specialists interested in the cyber ecosystem. The Cyber Career Pathways Tool resource presents a new and interactive way to explore Work Roles within the NICE Framework. It depicts the cyber workforce as five distinct, yet complementary, skill communities. It also highlights core attributes among each of the 52 Work Roles and offers actionable insights for employers, professionals, and individuals considering a career in cyber.[31]

SUMMARY

This chapter has provided a discussion of human resource and management approaches relative to the cybersecurity workforce, using the ELC model. The chapter began by considering how organizations recruit and hire talent, and how cybersecurity and federal employers specifically can attract the needed talent. In the section on talent advancement and development, the chapter examined training, certifications, conferences, and organizational culture.

Throughout this chapter, the committee considered aspects related to retention, the third level of the ELC model. This comprises both organizational characteristics that drive employee turnover and the role of compensation, including information on current compensation for cybersecurity talent. One aspect of retention addressed at length at various points in the chapter is compensation, which is an important component of talent management and retention for the FAA to consider. While it may be difficult for the FAA to directly compete with salaries from the private sector, the chapter reviews certain monetary incentives within their discretion that can be utilized. The committee also discussed cybersecurity talent retention and provides strategies not directly tied to compensation.

The committee also explored performance management strategies to cultivate cybersecurity competencies in the workforce. The section on talent development examined long-term initiatives that seek to support the growth of the cybersecurity workforce through the development of a hiring pipeline that involves cultivating cybersecurity talent in educational institutions. Finally, diversity is a necessary and integral part of any HR and management program. Throughout the chapter the committee considered special issues and challenges targeting diversity.

---

[31] This tool was created and is maintained in partnership with the Interagency Federal Cyber Career Pathways Working Group, led by CISA, the Department of Defense, and the Department of Veterans Affairs. Other tools and resources for current and future cybersecurity professionals can be found on CISA's National Initiative for Cybersecurity Careers and Studies website: https://niccs.cisa.gov/workforce-development/cyber-career-pathways.

Conclusions and Recommendations

CONCLUSION 3-1: The Federal Aviation Administration would benefit from engaging more robustly with recruitment fairs and college programs to bolster the hiring pipeline for cybersecurity positions.

CONCLUSION 3-2: "Early interest" is a notion that can be identified and then leveraged in recruitment. In the case of the Federal Aviation Administration, this includes not just an early interest in aviation, but also an early interest in cyber.

CONCLUSION 3-3: Long-term university partnerships using such activities as scholars-in-residence and fellowships from the Federal Aviation Administration might enhance the agency's ability to recruit talented recent college graduates.

CONCLUSION 3-4: In the case of the Federal Aviation Administration (FAA), there is a lack of clarity around what the marketing and branding are for promoting cybersecurity occupations, and there is a need for further identifying what the FAA could do to promote itself as an attractive/fulfilling/rewarding place for cybersecurity work.

CONCLUSION 3-5: The committee concludes that the use of numerical targets, such as number of the Scholarship for Service Program program graduates recruited and/or hired to internships and permanent employment, would be a useful mechanism for engaging additional interns with this program.

CONCLUSION 3-6: An optimal way of improving the cybersecurity workforce involves hiring employees with the right skill set and then reskilling them as the job requirements change. Two promising options for improving the cyber workforce in this fashion include programs such as the Scholarship for Service program or reskilling current employees.

The future FAA workforce will need skills and competencies, certifications, credentials, qualifications, career entry points, and career development pathways to achieve and sustain the mission of the FAA. In working to achieve and sustain such a workforce, the FAA will benefit from focused efforts in collaboration with educational institutions and the private sector, engagement in a wide variety of student and career development, and a well-rounded marketing effort that promotes the FAA as a desirable employer. Implementation of the following recommendations would help the FAA achieve its cybersecurity workforce goals.

RECOMMENDATION 3-1: The Federal Aviation Administration should evaluate the use of existing and future internship programs as valuable tools to create a more diverse cybersecurity workforce.

RECOMMENDATION 3-2: At the organizational level, promoting and marketing the agency as an attractive/fulfilling/rewarding place for cybersecurity would facilitate recruiting. However, there is a lack of clarity on what the Federal Aviation Administration's (FAA's) current marketing strategy and branding are for cybersecurity. While any FAA marketing approach needs to conform with the larger context of the brand of the federal government, actions to develop a strong FAA-specific marketing presence in cybersecurity should be implemented. To do so, the FAA should identify priority targets for recruitment (and identify their characteristics) and tailor their marketing to reach those targets effectively.

RECOMMENDATION 3-3: The Federal Aviation Administration (FAA) would benefit from engaging more robustly with recruitment fairs and college programs to bolster the hiring pipeline for cybersecurity positions. Moreover, long-term university partnerships using such activities as scholars-in-residence from the FAA might enhance the FAA's ability to recruit talented recent college graduates.

The FAA should organize and expand its reach and partnerships with universities around cybersecurity preparation efforts in academic and research areas to assist in the development of a talented cybersecurity workforce. Among these partnerships, the FAA should explore opportunities to develop meaningful and sustainable relationships with minority serving institutions[32] to access upcoming cybersecurity graduates via internships and employment opportunities.

RECOMMENDATION 3-4: Hiring employees with the right skill set and then growing them as the job requirements change is optimal. This is possible through programs such as the Scholarship for Service (SFS) program or reskilling current employees, which are two approaches for improving the cyber workforce. So far, the Federal Aviation Administration (FAA) has not partnered with the SFS program to effectively recruit cybersecurity talent to the organization; this is a missed opportunity and a partnership should be pursued. In this and other ways, the FAA should explore a wide range of options for meeting future reskilling needs, including internal, outside commercial, industry conference workshops, and outside rotations in agencies and industry.

RECOMMENDATION 3-5: Reskilling the existing workforce can be an important component of developing the needed future cybersecurity workforce for the Federal Aviation Administration and over time worker reskilling should grow beyond technical skills to include managerial and operational skills.

RECOMMENDATION 3-6: The Federal Aviation Administration should continue to use the National Initiative Cybersecurity Education tool to develop work roles that fit into a larger, well-designed organizational structure.

RECOMMENDATION 3-7: The Federal Aviation Administration should train its cyber leadership on best practices in building a diverse and inclusive organizational culture and should customize these best practices to implement a more contemporary culture.

RECOMMENDATION 3-8: When comparing nonsalary monetary incentives, the Federal Aviation Administration (FAA) cannot compete with industry pay scales. The FAA should leverage nonsalary monetary incentives (e.g., career development reimbursements, performance bonuses, etc.) as part of the overall compensation package.

RECOMMENDATION 3-9: "Early interest" in cybersecurity and in aviation by young students is a notion that can be identified and then leveraged in Federal Aviation Administration (FAA) recruitment. Two targeted actions are recommended here to foster and capitalize on FAA related "early interest":

- The FAA should review its past experience with effective fellowship and internship programs and also look to other federal agencies for proven models, such as the Department of Defense SMART scholarship program.
- The FAA should sponsor and leverage postsecondary-level cyber competitions.

REFERENCES

Acikgoz, Y. 2019. Employee recruitment and job search: Towards a multi-level integration. *Human Resource Management Review, 29*(1), 1–13.

---

[32]The U.S. Department of Education's Minority-Serving Institutions Program includes the following organizations: Historically Black Colleges and Universities (HBCUs); Hispanic-Serving Institutions (HSIs); Tribal Colleges and Universities (TCUs); and Asian American and Pacific Islander Serving Institutions (AAPISIs).

Acosta, J.C., McKee, J., Fielder, A., and Salamah, S. 2017. A Platform for Evaluator-Centric Cybersecurity Training and Data Acquisition. *MILCOM 2017–2017 IEEE Military Communications Conference (MILCOM)*, Baltimore, MD, pp. 393–399. doi: 10.1109/MILCOM.2017.8170768.

Adler, M., and Ziglio, E. 1996. *Gazing into the Oracle: The Delphi Method and Its Application to Social Policy and Public Health*. London: Kingsley Publishers.

Amankwah-Amoah, J. 2015. An integrative review of the antecedents and consequences of lateral hiring. *Journal of Management Development, 34*(7), 754–772.

Baer, M.D., Bundy, J., Garud, N., and Kim, J.K. 2018. The benefits and burdens of organizational reputation for employee well-being: A conservation of resources approach. *Personnel Psychology, 71*(4), 571–595.

Bishop, M. 2004. *Introduction to Computer Security*. Boston, MA: Pearson Education, Inc.

Burrell, D.N. 2018. An exploration of the cybersecurity workforce shortage. *International Journal of Hyperconnectivity and the Internet of Things, 2*(1), 29–41. doi: 10.4018/IJHIoT.2018010103.

Burke, M. ND. *Six Stages to Success with the Employee Lifecycle*. 6Q. Available: https://inside.6q.io/six-stages-to-success-with-the-employee-lifecycle/.

Caulkins, B.D., Badillo-Urquiola, K., Bockelman, P., and Leis, R. 2016. Cyber Workforce Development Using a Behavioral Cybersecurity Paradigm. *2016 International Conference on Cyber Conflict (CyCon U.S.)*, Washington, DC, pp. 1–6. doi: 10.1109/CYCONUS.2016.7836614.

Champion, M., Jariwala, S., Ward, P., and Cooke, N.J. 2014. Using Cognitive Task Analysis to Investigate the Contribution of Informational Education to Developing Cyber Security Expertise. *Proceedings of the Human Factors and Ergonomics Society Annual Meeting, 58*, Philadelphia, PA, pp. 310–314.

Chapman, D.S., Uggerslev, K.L., Carroll, S.A., Piasentin, K.A., and Jones, D.A. 2005. Applicant attraction to organizations and job choice: A meta-analytic review of the correlates of recruiting outcomes. *Journal of Applied Psychology, 90*(5), 928.

CISA (Cybersecurity and Infrastructure Security Agency). 2019. Cybersecurity Talent Identification and Assessment. January. Available: https://niccs.cisa.gov/sites/default/files/documents/pdf/cybersecurity%20talent%20identification%20and%20assessment.pdf?trackDocs=cybersecurity%20talent%20identification%20and%20assessment.pdf.

Collins, C.J., and Stevens, C.K. 2002. The relationship between early recruitment-related activities and the application decisions of new labor-market entrants: A brand equity approach to recruitment. *Journal of Applied Psychology, 87*(6), 1121.

Cook. S. 2020. "The Cybersecurity Imperative." Presentation to Committee on Cybersecurity Workforce of the Federal Aviation Administration. April 23, 2020. Virtual meeting.

Coovert, M.D., Wiernik, B., and Martin, J. 2020. *Use of Technology-Enhanced Simulations for Cyber Aptitude Assessment: Phase II Prototype Development*. Technical Report, Accession Number: AD1107016. Fort Belvoir, VA: Defense Technical Information Center.

Coovert, M.D., Wiernik, B., and Martin, J. 2019. *Use of Technology-Enhanced Simulations for Cyber Aptitude Assessment*. Technical Report. Plant City, FL: MDC & Associates.

Coovert, M.D., Winner, J., Bennett, W., and Howard, D.J. 2017. Serious games are a serious tool for team research. *International Journal of Serious Games, 4*(1). doi: 10.17083/ijsg.v4i1.141.

Coull, N., Donald, I., Ferguson, I., Keane, E., Mitchell, T. Smith, O.V., Stevenson, E., and Tomkins, P. 2017. The gamification of cybersecurity training. International conference on technologies for e-learning and digital entertainment. Edutainment 2017. *Lecture Notes in Computer Science, 10345*, 108–111. doi: 10.1007/978-3-319-65849-0_13.

Cropanzano, R., Bowen, D.E., and Gilliland, S.W. 2007. The management of organizational justice. *Academy of Management Perspectives, 21*(4), 24–48.

Crumpler, W., and Lewis, J.A. 2019. *Cybersecurity Workforce Gap*. Washington, DC: Center for Strategic and International Studies.

Darnold, T.C., and Rynes, S.L. 2013. Recruitment and Job Choice Research: Same as It Ever Was? Pp. 103–143 in *Handbook of Psychology: Volume 12 Industrial and Organizational Psychology* (I.B. Weiner, N.W. Schmitt, and S. Highhouse, eds.). Hoboken, NJ: John Wiley and Sons, Inc.

DeNisi, A.S., and Murphy, K.R. 2017. Performance appraisal and performance management: 100 years of progress? *Journal of Applied Psychology, 102*(3), 421.

DeNisi, A.S., and Pritchard, R.D. 2006. Performance appraisal, performance management and improving individual performance: A motivational framework. *Management and Organization Review, 2*(2), 253–277.

DHS (Department of Homeland Security). 2016. *Cybersecurity Workforce Development Toolkit: How to Build a Strong Cybersecurity Workforce*. Available: https://niccs.cisa.gov/sites/default/files/documents/pdf/cybersecurity_workforce_development_toolkit.pdf?trackDocs=cybersecurity_workforce_development_toolkit.pdf.7/978-3-319-77028-4_20.

Domínguez, M., Prada, M.A., Reguera, P., Fuertes, J.J., Alonso, S., and Morán, A. 2017. Cybersecurity training in control systems using real equipment. *IFAC-PapersOnLine, 50*(1), 12179–12184.

Dreibelbis, R.C., Martin, J., Coovert, M.D., and Dorsey, D.W. 2018. The looming cybersecurity crisis and what it means for the practice of industrial and organizational psychology. *Industrial and Organizational Psychology, 11*(2), 346–365.

Embry, J. 2020. "U.S. Coast Guard." Presentation to Committee on Cybersecurity Workforce of the Federal Aviation Administration. June 29, 2020. Virtual meeting.

Erez, M., and Kanfer, F.H.. 1983. The role of goal acceptance in goal setting and task performance. *Academy of Management Review, 8*(3), 454–463.

Gestwicki, P., and Stumbaugh, K. 2015. Observations and opportunities in cybersecurity education game design. *2015 Computer Games: AI, Animation, Mobile, Multimedia, Educational and Serious Games (CGAMES)*, Louisville, KY, pp. 131–137. doi: 10.1109/CGames.2015.7272970.

Harris, C., Brown, L.W., and Wright, P. 2020. If You Spend It, They Will Come: Recruiting Expenses, Reputation, and Human Capital Acquisition. P. 13282 In *Academy of Management Proceedings* (Vol. 2020, No. 1). Briarcliff Manor, NY: Academy of Management.

Hernandez, S. 2020. "Government Cyber Workforce Challenges." Presentation to Committee on Cybersecurity Workforce of the Federal Aviation Administration. February 20, 2020. Washington, DC.

Huynh D., Luong P., Iida H., and Beuran, R. 2017. Design and Evaluation of a Cybersecurity Awareness Training Game. Pp. 183–188 in *Entertainment Computing – ICEC 2017. Lecture Notes in Computer Science, vol 10507* (N. Munekata, I. Kunita, and J. Hoshino, eds.). Cham: Springer. doi: 10.1007/978-3-319-66715-7_19.

Ilgen, D.R., and Feldman, J.M. 1983. Performance appraisal: A process focus. *Research in Organizational Behavior*, 5, 141–197.

Inderrieden, E.J., Keaveny, T.J., and Allen, R.E. 1988. Predictors of employee satisfaction with the performance appraisal process. *Journal of Business and Psychology*, 2(4), 306–310.

Jackson, S.E., and Joshi, A. 2004. Diversity is social context: A multi-attribute, multilevel analysis of team diversity and sales performance. *Diversity and the Workplace*, 25(6), 675–702.

Jacob, J., Wei, W. Sha, K., Davari, S., and Yang, T.A. 2018. Is the NICE Cybersecurity Workforce Framework (NCWF) Effective for a Workforce Comprising of Interdisciplinary Majors? *Proceedings of the 16th International Conference on Scientific Computing (CSC'18)*, Las Vegas, NV, pp. 124–130.

JTF (Joint Task Force on Cybersecurity Education). 2017. *Cybersecurity Curricula 2017 Curriculum Guidelines for Post-Secondary Degree Programs in Cybersecurity*. A Report in the Computing Curricula Series Joint Task Force on Cybersecurity Education. Available: https://www.acm.org/binaries/content/assets/education/curricula-recommendations/csec2017.pdf.

Justice, C., and Vyas, R. 2017. Cybersecurity Education: Runlabs Rapidly Create Virtualized Labs Based on a Simple Configuration File. *American Society for Engineering Education Annual Conference and Exposition, Conference Proceedings*, Columbus, OH, paper ID 18888.

Katsantonis, M.N., Fouliras, P., and Mavridis, J. 2017. Conceptualization of Game Based Approaches for Learning and Training on Cyber Security. *PCI 2017: Proceedings of the 21st Pan-Hellenic Conference on Informatics*, *36*, Larissa, Greece, pp. 1–2. doi: 10.1145/3139367.3139415.

Kempinksi, R., and Cunningham, L. 2020. "Recruiting Mission-Critical Cyber Personnel." Presentation to Committee on Cybersecurity Workforce of the Federal Aviation Administration. September 16, 2020. Virtual meeting.

Kim, T., and Holzer, M. 2016. Public employees and performance appraisal: A study of antecedents to employees' perception of the process. *Review of Public Personnel Administration*, 36(1), 31–56.

Knapp, K.J., Maurer, C., and Planchkinova, M. 2017. Maintaining a cybersecurity curriculum: professional certifications as valuable guidance. *Journal of Information Systems Education, 28*(2), 101–114.

Kristof-Brown, A.L., Zimmerman, R.D., and Johnson, E.C. 2005. Consequences of individuals' fit at work: A meta-analysis of person-job, person-organization, person-group, and person-supervisor fit. *Personnel Psychology, 58*, 643–672.

Lawong, D., Ferris, G.R., Hochwarter, W., and Maher, L. 2019. *Recruiter Political Skill and Organization Reputation Effects on Job Applicant Attraction in the Recruitment Process*. Career Development International. Available: https://www.researchgate.net/publication/335267146_Recruiter_political_skill_and_organization_reputation_effects_on_job_applicant_attraction_in_the_recruitment_process_A_multi-study_investigation.

Le Blanc, K., and Freeman, S. 2016. Investigating the Relationship between Need for Cognition and Skill in Ethical Hackers. Pp. 223–228 in *Advances in Human Factors in Cybersecurity. Advances in Intelligent Systems and Computing, vol 501* (D. Nicholson, ed.). Cham: Springer.

Lewis, A. 2020. "Industry Cyber Workforce Challenges." Presentation to Committee on Cybersecurity Workforce of the Federal Aviation Administration. February 20, 2020. Washington, DC.

Li, C., and Kulkarni, R. 2016. Survey of Cybersecurity Education through Gamification. *2016 American Society for Engineering Education Annual Conference and Exposition*, New Orleans, LA, paper ID 16728.

Liggans, G., Attoh, P., Gong, T., Chase, T., Clark, P., and Russell, M. 2018. Diversity and inclusion efforts in federal agencies: A context for exploring perceptions of military veterans. *Journal of Veterans Studies, 3*(1), 139–151. doi: 10.21061/jvs.v3i1.48.

Lowenstein, M.W. 2017. *Employee Ambassadorship: Optimizing Customer-Centric Behavior from the Inside-Out and Outside-In*. New York: Business Expert Press.

Mack, N.A., Cummings, R., Womack, K., Dowling, N., Huff, Jr., E.W., and Gosha, K. 2019. From Midshipmen to Cyber Pros: Training Minority Naval Reserve Officer Training Corp Students for Cybersecurity. *Proceedings of the 50th ACM Technical Symposium on Computer Science Education*, Minneapolis, MN, pp. 726–730.

Mannix, E., and Neale, M.A. 2005. What differences make a difference?: The promise and reality of diverse teams in organizations. *Psychological Science in the Public Interest, 6*(2), 31–55.

Marinos, N. 2017. *Cybersecurity: Federal Efforts are Underway That May Address Workforce Challenges*. Washington, DC: United States Government Accountability Office.

Martinaityte, I., Sacramento, C., and Aryee, S. 2019. Delighting the customer: Creativity-oriented high-performance work systems, frontline employee creative performance, and customer satisfaction. *Journal of Management, 45*(2), 728–751.

McGettrick, A., Cassel, L.N., Dark, M., Hawthorne, E.K., and Impagliazzo, J. 2014. Toward Curricular Guidelines for Cybersecurity. *Proceedings of the 45th ACM Technical Symposium on Computer Science Education (SIGCSE '14)*, New York, NY, pp. 81–82. doi: 10.1145/2538862.2538990.

Mendelberg, T., Karpowitz, C., and Oliphant, J. 2014. Gender inequality in deliberation: Unpacking the black box of interaction. *Perspectives on Politics, 12*(1), 18–44. doi: 10.1017/S1537592713003691.

Meyer, H.H., Kay, E., and French, J.R. 1981. Split Roles in Performance Appraisal. Pp. 70–84 in *Psychology and Industrial Productivity* (M.M. Gruneberg, and D.J. Oborne, eds.). London: Palgrave Macmillan.

Morgan, S. 2017. Cybersecurity Labor Crunch to Hit 3.5 Million Unfilled Jobs by 2021. *Cybersecurity Business Report*. Available: https://www.csoonline.com/article/3200024/cybersecurity-labor-crunch-to-hit-35-million-unfilled-jobs-by-2021.html.

Murphy, K.R., and Cleveland, J.N. 1991. *Performance Appraisal: An Organizational Perspective*. Boston, MA: Allyn & Bacon.

NASEM (National Academies of Sciences, Engineering, and Medicine). 2019. *Minority Serving Institutions: America's Underutilized Resource for Strengthening the STEM Workforce*. Washington, DC: The National Academies Press.

NASEM. 2018. *Assessing and Responding to the Computer Science Undergraduate Enrollments*. Washington, DC: The National Academies Press.

NASEM. 2017. *Foundational Cybersecurity Research: Improving Science, Engineering, and Institutions*. Washington, DC: The National Academies Press. doi: 10.17226/24676.

NRC (National Research Council). 2013. *Professionalizing the Nation's Cybersecurity Workforce? Criteria for Decision-Making*. Washington, DC: The National Academies Press.

Nessi, D. 2020. "Building a Cybersecurity Team: The Airport Perspective." Presentation to Committee on Cybersecurity Workforce of the Federal Aviation Administration. June 30, 2020. Virtual meeting.

Newhouse, W. Keith, S., Scribner, B., and Witte, G. 2017. *National Initiative for Cybersecurity Education (NICE) Cybersecurity Workforce Framework*. NIST Special Publication 800-181. Gaithersburg, MD: National Institute of Standards and Technology. doi: 10.6028/NIST.SP.800-181.

Ng, E.S., and Sears, G.J. 2017. The glass ceiling in context: The influence of CEO gender, recruitment practices and firm internationalization on the representation of women in management. *Human Resource Management Journal, 27*(1), 133–151.

Oltsik, J. 2017. *Research Report: The Life and Times of Cybersecurity Professionals*. The Enterprise Strategy Group, Inc., and Information Systems Security Association International. Available: https://www.esg-global.com/hubfs/issa/ESG-ISSA-Research-Report-Life-of-Cybersecurity-Professionals-Nov-2017.pdf.

OMB (Office of Management and Budget). 2016. *Memorandum for Heads of Executive Department and Agencies M-16-15: Federal Cybersecurity Workforce Strategy*. Available: https://www.whitehouse.gov/sites/whitehouse.gov/files/omb/memoranda/2016/m-16-15.pdf.

Page, S. 2019. *The Diversity Bonus: How Great Teams Pay Off in the Knowledge Economy*. Princeton, NJ: Princeton University Press.

Pelt, D.H.M., van der Linden, D., Dunkel, C.S., and Born, M.P. 2017. The general factor of personality and job performance: Revisiting previous meta-analyses. *International Journal Selection and Assessment, 25*, 333–346. doi: 10.1111/ijsa.12188.

Perez, J. 2020. "UPS Cybersecurity Defense In-Depth Strategy." Presentation to Committee on Cybersecurity Workforce of the Federal Aviation Administration. June 29, 2020. Virtual meeting.

Piotrowski, V. 2020. "CyberCorps® Scholarship for Service Program (SFS)." Presentation to Committee on Cybersecurity Workforce of the Federal Aviation Administration. April 22, 2020. Virtual meeting.

Pulakos, E.D., Mueller-Hanson, R., and Arad, S. 2019. The evolution of performance management: Searching for value. *Annual Review of Organizational Psychology and Organizational Behavior, 6*, 249–271. doi: 10.1146/annurev orgpsych-012218-015009.

Reed, J., and Acosta-Rubio, J. 2018. *Innovation Through Inclusion: The Multicultural Cybersecurity Workforce. An (ISC)² Global Information Security Workforce Study*. (ISC)². Available: https://www.isc2.org/-/media/Files/Research/Innovation-Through-Inclusion-Report.ashx.

Resick, C.J., Baltes, B.B., and Shantz, C.W. 2007. Person-organization fit and work-related attitudes and decisions: Examining interactive effects with job fit and conscientiousness. *Journal of Applied Psychology, 92*(5), 1446–1455. doi: 10.1037/0021-9010.92.5.1446.

Reynolds, D., and Dickter, D.N. 2017. Technology and Employee Selection: An Overview. Pp. 855–873 in *Handbook of Employee Selection* (2nd ed.) (J.L. Farr, and N.T. Tippins, eds.). New York: Routledge.

Santos, O. 2019. *Developing Cybersecurity Programs and Policies*. London, UK: Pearson Education, Inc.

Santos, D., Goel, S., Costanzo, J., Sagan, D., and Buddelmeyer, P. 2020. *A Roadmap for Successful Regional Alliances and Multistakeholder Partnerships to Build the Cybersecurity Workforce*. NISTIR 8287. Gaithersburg, MD: National Institute of Standards and Technology.

Schneider, F.B. 2013. Cybersecurity education in universities. *IEEE Security & Privacy, 11*(4), 3–4. doi: 10.1109/MSP.2013.84.

Siraj, A. 2020. "Towards Gender Balance CyberSecurity Workforce." Presentation to Committee on Cybersecurity Workforce of the Federal Aviation Administration. April 23, 2020. Virtual meeting.

Smith-Doerr, L., Alegria, S.N., and Sacco, T. 2017. How diversity matters in the US science and engineering workforce: A critical review considering integration in teams, fields, and organizational contexts. *Engaging Science, Technology, and Society, 3*, 139–153.

Smither, J.W., and London, M. 2009. *Performance Management: Putting Research into Action*. Vol. 21. San Francisco, CA: Josey-Bass.

Spidalieri, F., and McArdle, J. 2016. Transforming the next generation of military leaders into cyber-strategic leaders: The role of cybersecurity education in US service academies. *The Cyber Defense Review, Spring*, 141–163.

Tadmor, C.T., Satterstrom, P., Jang, S., and Polzer, J.T. 2012. Beyond individual creativity: The superadditive benefits of multicultural experience for collective creativity in culturally diverse teams. *Journal of Cross-Cultural Psychology, 43*(3), 383–392.

Tioh, J.-N., Mina, M., and Jacobson, D. 2017. Cyber Security Training: A Survey of Serious Games in Cyber Security. *Institute of Electrical and Electronics Engineers Frontiers in Education Conference, 1*, Indianapolis, IN, pp. 1–5.

Tippins, N., Sackett, P., and Oswald, F. 2018. Principles for the validation and use of personnel selection procedures. *Industrial and Organizational Psychology, 11*(S1), 1–97.

Tisu, L., Lupșa, D., Vîrgă, D., and Rusu, A. 2020. Personality characteristics, job performance and mental health: The mediating role of work engagement. *Personality and Individual Differences, 153*. doi: 10.1016/j.paid.2019.109644.

Turner, D. 2021. Vets facing difficult transition to civilian jobs. *Stars and Stripes*. Available: https://www.military.com/veteran-jobs/career-advice/job-hunting/vets-facing-difficult-transition-to-civilian-jobs.html.

Urias, V.E., Van Leeuwen, B., Stout W.M.S., and Lin, H.W. 2017. Dynamic Cybersecurity Training Environments for an Evolving Cyber Workforce. In *2017 IEEE International Symposium on Technologies for Homeland Security (HST)*, Waltham, MA, pp. 1–6. doi: 10.1109/THS.2017.7943509.

Vogel, R. 2016. Closing the cybersecurity skills gap. *Salus Journal, 4*(2), 32–46. doi: 10.3316/informit.093144667545339.

Wang, P., and D'Cruze, H. 2019. Certification in cybersecurity workforce development: A case study. *International Journal of Hyperconnectivity and the Internet of Things (IJHIoT), 3*(2), 38–57.

Wang, J., Cheng, G.H.L., Chen, T., and Leung, K. 2019. Team creativity/innovation in culturally diverse teams: A meta-analysis. *Journal of Organizational Behavior, 40*(6), 693–708.

Weber, L. 2019. Why Companies are Failing at Reskilling. *Wall Street Journal*, April 19.

Welbourne, T.M., Rolf, S., and Schlachter, S. 2017. The case for employee resource groups: A review and social identify theory-based research agenda. *Personnel Review, 46*(8), 1816–1834. doi: 10.1108/PR-01-2016-0004.

Worden, M., and Romero, H. 2020. "Raytheon Cyber and Aviation Security." Presentation to Committee on Cybersecurity Workforce of the Federal Aviation Administration. April 23, 2020. Virtual meeting.

Wright, M. 2015. Improving cybersecurity workforce capacity and capability. *Information Systems Security Association International Journal, 13*(10), 13–20.

Yang, L-Q., Levine, E.L., Smith, M.A., Ispas, D., and Rossi, M.E. 2008. Person-environment fit or person plus environment: A meta-analysis of studies using polynomial regression analysis. *Human Resources Management Review, 18*(4), 311–321.

4

Additional Employee and Organizational Considerations

INTRODUCTION

A diverse cybersecurity workforce has become an increasingly critical component of public and private organizations, including the Federal Aviation Administration (FAA). This chapter continues the discussion begun in Chapter 3 of the employee lifecycle (ELC) model by turning to a consideration of the third and fourth stages of the ELC: Retention and Retirement. The committee first describes opportunities for the FAA's talent retention, talent pipeline development, and retirement. The chapter concludes by highlighting public and private best practices in cybersecurity organizational structure, cybersecurity skill taxonomies, cybersecurity sourcing, and inclusion in the cybersecurity program.

RETENTION

The retention stage of the ELC model addresses how organizations can ensure their workplace remains attractive to their skilled employees. This includes looking at the factors driving employee turnover, among them the role of compensation in either retaining current employees or incentivizing them to leave for other opportunities. Employee turnover is a major concern for nearly half of the managers who belong to the Society for Human Resource Management (SHRM), the primary professional organization for human resource professionals (SHRM, 2018). This focus on turnover is due at least in part to the cost associated with hiring replacement employees. The replacement cost can be estimated between 90 and 200 percent of annual salary (Allen et al., 2010).

One of the first research-based models to explain employee turnover was developed by Mobley (1977). Mobley established a linkage between psychological withdrawal (e.g., thinking of quitting), behavioral indicators (e.g., increased absenteeism, tardiness), and the turnover behavior itself. External factors, such as the availability of alternative jobs, also influence an employee's decision to leave an organization. Subsequent research on turnover led to the identification of other important attitudes held by employees, including organizational commitment, engagement, perception of being treated fairly by the organization (Narayanan et al., 2019), and empowerment.

An unfolding model of turnover was developed by Lee and Mitchell (1994). According to this model, turnover is characterized by four distinct paths, each with distinct foci, psychological processes, and external influences. These authors make a case that turnover can be triggered by critical events, such as an unexpected job offer, spouse or family influence, and social abuse (e.g., bullying from supervision or peers) on the job. Fit models (introduced in Chapter 3) are also useful in explaining the accumulation (or lack) of dissatisfaction on the part of the employee. The better an individual's knowledge, skills, abilities, and other characteristics (KSAOs) fit the requirements of the job, the work team, and organization, the more satisfied (less dissatisfied) the individual is (Lee and Mitchell, 1994; Subramony, 2009; Wolfson and Mathieu, 2018). As retention is influenced by each of these factors, each factor needs to be monitored and appropriately neutralized or countered (e.g., an outside job offer receives a counteroffer).

The process of managing employee retention in the committee's judgment needs to be evidence-based. Surveys are often useful in capturing attitudinal measures such as job satisfaction and organizational commitment. Similarly, job, team, and organizational fit can be measured via surveys and/or during the developmental phase of an annual (or more frequent) performance appraisal (Borman et al., 1997; Krumm and Hertel, 2013; Levy et al., 2011). To the extent possible, it is advisable that job satisfaction, organizational commitment, fit, and alternative job availability be monitored as frequently as possible (e.g., 3–4 times per year) using analytics and statistical analysis to model individual and group trends, and acting when necessary to counter or neutralize pressures that tend to increase turnover. The organization also needs to be sensitive to generational differences as certain groups, such as millennials, are often motivated by and hold different values than other generations. Generational differences need to be identified and managed along with traditional constructs associated with retention or turnover, such as satisfaction, commitment, and fit measures (including P-O, or person-organization fit; P-J, or person-job fit; P-T, or person-team fit).

Based on a meta-analysis of the turnover literature, Lee and colleagues (2018) developed a typology of four classes of individuals who stay/turnover. The four types of individuals described below should receive different targeted interventions as retention strategies. Some stay in the organization because they want to and can stay (enthusiastic stayers—job is fulfilling and has good fit indices); and those who want to leave the organization and have the ability to do so (enthusiastic leavers—have other jobs available to them). A third group wants to stay but they must leave (reluctant leavers—for example are let go during a downturn in the economy), and those who want to leave but must stay (reluctant stayers—e.g., family/spouse constraints inhibit leaving). It is straightforward to see how individuals in each group would require and respond to alternative internal and external motivation and retention strategies. Similarly, a close examination of satisfaction and embeddedness surveys for each group might reveal important issues relative to turnover. For example, the organization might ascertain it is top-heavy in reluctant stayers, resulting in productivity issues. In the committee interviews with FAA employees, there were discussions of losing younger cyber talent during government furloughs.[1] These employees were reluctant to leave but needed to as they had to support themselves and their families.[2]

Compensation

According to salary.com,[3] the average information security (IS) and cybersecurity salary is $106,972 as of July 2020.[4] The 2020 Cybersecurity Salary Survey looks at five positions: Security Analyst/Threat Intelligence Specialist, Security Architect/Cloud Security Architect, Penetration Tester, Network Security Engineering, and Security Director/Manager (Cynet, 2020). The survey looks at salaries, relative organizational impacts (e.g., geolocation, industry, etc.), and individual factors (e.g., gender, experience, certification). According to the survey, location matters with salaries being higher in the United States than in other continents. Bonuses were also common except among Security Analysts, ranging between 1 and 10 percent per year. Another finding was that a degree does not guarantee a higher salary; among those surveys, similar salary ranges were found for those with and without a college degree.

In addition to salary, other benefits cybersecurity employees are looking for can be hard to measure; these include the ability to learn on the job; access to a senior person/being a senior person; training resources; potential for contribution/change; organizational culture, organizational fit, and organizational support to retain cybersecurity talent; a cybersecurity vision or strategy; rewards for employees; and leadership for good cybersecurity (Zurko, 2020).

---

[1] Focus group discussion with FAA managers and committee members, August 21, 2020. All discussions were conducted in confidentiality, and the names of the participants are withheld by mutual agreement.

[2] Focus group discussion with FAA managers and committee members, August 21, 2020.

[3] More information is available at: https://www.salary.com/research/salary/posting/information-systems-and-cybersecurity-salary.

[4] More information is also available at the U.S. Bureau of Labor Statistics for Occupational Employment and Wage statistics. Data can be found at http://www.bls.org.

Raw pay gaps are driven mainly by compensable factors, with a smaller portion driven by unexplained pay inequities (Greenfield, 2020). From Greenfield's presentation, the committee learned that the single most important factor determining an employee's pay is their career level or salary grade (i.e., where they sit in an organization's hierarchy). Thus, closing raw pay gaps will require organizations to ensure women and people of color gain access to more senior, higher-paying roles. However, even small, unexplained pay gaps deserve attention. A back-of-the-envelope calculation suggests that a 1¢ unexplained pay gap translates into lost wages for women in the U.S. economy of roughly $500 million each week (Greenfield, 2020). Best practices for pay equity include using a robust statistical approach to assess pay equity; having a formalized remediation process to address identified pay equity risks; having an assigned team responsible for conducting pay equity assessment; and enforcing pay equity policies and practices (Greenfield, 2020).

Finding 4-1: Compensation is an important component of talent management and retention for the FAA to consider. While it may be difficult for the FAA to directly compete with salaries from the private sector, certain monetary incentives can be utilized. Aligned with compensation, cyber talent retention and strategies not directly tied to compensation can be attractive to the cyber employee.

In her presentation to the committee, Jamie Embry described how the Coast Guard provides substantial hiring bonuses and retention bonuses to ensure they can attract and retain a sufficient cyber workforce (Embry, 2020). Another tool described by Embry is the ability to gain certifications on the job, which helps train the workforce and serves as an incentive because it supports career development.

There are many constructs[5] an organization should be aware of and monitor to keep employees retained. It is important to monitor these via surveys, interviews, and other strategies to gather attitudinal and behavioral data (Lee and Mitchell, 2003). The data should be gathered and statistically analyzed so both long-term and short-term trends are identified at the individual and group levels (Hom et al., 1992). When negative trends (e.g., a rising level of dissatisfaction) emerge, action should be taken to mitigate factors leading to dissatisfaction. Similarly, if an enthusiastic leaver receives a job offer, efforts should be made to counter (Li et al., 2016a).

Workplace flexibility is a powerful tool for talent retention, and changes in telecommuting opportunities related to the COVID-19 pandemic have become an increasingly important issue for employees. Work-life balance is an important factor for many younger employees and is increasingly important for all employees (Singh, 2019). Flexible work schedules and flexibility in work location may be a way to bring talent to less desirable locations. Organizations experiencing difficulty recruiting employees due to work locations should consider allowing telecommuting for job roles that do not require employees to be on site.

Career Advancement and Development

Several of the presenters in the data-gathering sessions indicated the importance of perceived merit in hiring and retention practices. For example, technical cybersecurity professionals may not be motivated in an environment where seniority guides career development. In addition to favoring merit-based advancement, other factors that are important to technical professionals in the cybersecurity fields are that they find their work challenging and interesting, they have sufficient resources to do their work well, and they have career advancement opportunities. In the committee's conversations with cybersecurity professionals in the FAA, the individuals indicated that they often feel that, due to a lack of resources, the issues they find in the security of their systems cannot be resolved.[6] Additionally, the professionals expressed that they felt that sometimes management listened more to contractors than the full-time employees and involved contractors in decision making while excluding FAA employees.[7]

---

[5]Per https://dictionary.apa.org, a construct is a complex idea or concept formed from a synthesis of simpler ideas.

[6]Focus group discussion with FAA employees and committee members, August 20, 2020. All discussions were conducted in confidentiality, and the names of the participants are withheld by mutual agreement. Focus group discussion with FAA managers and committee members, August 21, 2020.

[7]Focus group discussion with FAA employees and committee members, August 20, 2020.

Appreciation

As reviewed above, several factors impact the retention of individuals in an organization. External and motivational factors are differentially important, depending on why an individual is considering leaving an organization (e.g., reluctant stayers/leavers). One motivational factor of increasing research importance is appreciation. Simply stated, individuals who feel appreciated are less likely to turn over than those to whom the organization does not convey the same information about the person's worth to the organization and its goals. This importance is likely due to appreciation and recognition being considered innate human needs (Abdullah et al., 2016).

Research examining the role of appreciation at work and its importance to outcomes such as increased job satisfaction and decreased turnover is growing. For example, a longitudinal design covering six Swiss organizations found appreciation to be central in employees' feelings of success in the organization, satisfaction with the job, and overall satisfaction with the organization (Pfister et al., 2020). Similarly, Abdulla and colleagues (2016) demonstrate appreciation (along with recognition) to be central in job satisfaction for Malaysian IT workers. Even in situations where a worker might believe a work task is unnecessary, unreasonable, or outside the scope of their responsibilities (termed *illegitimate task* in the research literature), an individual is more likely to complete the task if they feel appreciated. Muntz and Dormann (2020) demonstrate this in a longitudinal study of nurses. Their conclusions highlight that nurses who felt appreciated were less likely to perceive a task as illegitimate; it generally costs organizations little to create an environment of appreciation and it is "highly powerful" (p. 391).

But what is appreciation? At one level, appreciation is something we all know. A person can both feel appreciated and also rationally consider whether they are appreciated by an organization. Researchers such as Fagley (2012, 2016) and Fagley and Adler (2012) are more clearly defining the construct space of appreciation by arguing it has eight specific facets. Fagley (2016) defines these aspects as:

1. "Have" focus: Focusing on, and valuing, what one has.
2. Awe: Feeling awe or wonder in response to nature, beauty, or life itself.
3. Ritual: Using routines or practices to foster noticing and valuing something (appreciation).
4. Present Moment: Focusing on the present moment and valuing it.
5. Self or Social Comparison: Using self or social comparisons to promote appreciation.
6. Gratitude: Feeling grateful to a benefactor for help, support, or opportunities.
7. Loss or Adversity: Appreciation (noticing and valuing something) triggered by experiences of loss or adversity.
8. Interpersonal: Noticing and valuing the people in one's life.

Identifying particular aspects of appreciation and the importance each plays in an individual's work life offers opportunities for the FAA to foster a sense of appreciation in its cyber employees. For example, the FAA could communicate to individuals the "Haves" in their job (e.g., access to cutting-edge technology, tools, and training), or the "Awe" or "Social Comparison" aspects of being able to work for the premier aviation organization in the world. Of course any of the other aspects of appreciation could be utilized by the FAA as well. The outcome for the FAA of increasing perceptions of appreciation would include increased job satisfaction and less turnover among its cybersecurity workforce.

FAA RETENTION

Due to the shortage of qualified cybersecurity talent, unemployment rates for this workforce population are low to non-existent. Thus, recruitment remains a challenge. However, forward-thinking organizations, in the midst of a recruitment battle, have begun to use more systems-level approaches to both recruit and better *retain* cybersecurity talent. Without effective retention practices, recruitment becomes a revolving door, and cost management becomes an issue due to the need to continue to orient and train new talent. Retention is a challenge faced by the FAA cybersecurity workforce, and in the committee meetings the FAA personnel discussed several barriers to retention, including (FAA, 2020):

- A growing proportion of retirement eligible personnel;
- Fast-paced changes in cybersecurity threats and vulnerabilities that require employees to acquire new knowledge on a consistent basis;
- Competition with private industry, the Department of Defense, and intelligence agencies;
- Preferences of workers to go to contract positions due to salary limitations (the general schedule grades and steps) in FAA jobs;
- Noncompetitiveness of salaries; and
- Limited opportunities for advancement because of policies around time-in-rank.

Based on discussions with the sponsor and the committee, the turnover rate of FAA employees is lower than other agencies, but the rising need for cybersecurity talent, and more so, a diverse and talented workforce intensifies the need to focus on retention. Often, organizations separate recruitment efforts from retention efforts, yet a systems view reveals that they are highly interdependent and that it is important to integrate the two (Schweyer, 2004). Every recruitment initiative should be strongly integrated with retention initiatives, and prospective employees should be provided with retention incentives.

The committee's literature review found that experts in the field of employee retention have grounded forward-thinking best practices for retention in three primary areas: (1) ensuring employees can build human capital in the workplace; (2) focusing on management practices and attitudes as leading indicators of employee intent to depart from an organization; and (3) advancing workplace culture to enhance the attractiveness of the organization for both recruitment *and* retention. Many of these scholars mention the need to increase workforce diversity simply due to the changing demographics of the United States. Likewise, there is a strong need to increase the heterogeneity of talent, skills, and knowledge to address complex problems, especially in cybersecurity. Thus, best practices provided here assume an integrated systems approach to recruitment and retention, as well as an authentic commitment to diversity and inclusion within the FAA.

Human Capital in the Workplace

Fundamentally, retention of employees rests on their perceptions of the likelihood of moving to higher and suitable positions within the workplace. This often involves human capital development, which is an expanding practice in organizations to attract and retain talented workers. Alnachef and Alhajjar (2015) define the practice as "helping people to acquire expertise" (p. 1154). Effective human capital development is grounded in a systematic, strategic plan to grow employees' professional capabilities and to understand employees' current needs and future aspirations within the organization (Alnachef and Alhajjar, 2015).

Human capital development has also been conceptualized as a social capital development process. Etti (2020) posits a human capital model to attract and retain women and ethnic minorities in the U.S. Federal Civil Service. The model is adapted from several scholars focusing on the role of social capital in organizations (Bourdieu, 1989; Coleman, 1988; Cross and Cummings, 2004; Granovetter, 1973). The model posits several interconnected factors necessary for organizations to assist employees in developing human capital. In this regard, the leader-member exchange between managers and employees can be strengthened and ultimately result in positive impacts on retention. The model has been adapted in Figure 4-1 to include more concepts specific to the FAA and cybersecurity.

Etti builds on work by Alnachef and Alhajjar (2015), who proposed an initial model to address many of the same human capital concepts depicted in Figure 4-1 (Etti, 2020). In their initial model, Alnachef and Alhajjar identified three actions any employer can build into the organizational culture to grow and retain strong talent: (1) provide employees with relevant opportunities for learning and education; (2) consistently support the development of experience and expertise; and (3) create and implement opportunities to grow employees' innovation and creativity (p. 1156).

Naff (1994) highlighted the limited advancement of women in civil service positions. Lack of human capital due to formal education or experiential learning opportunities as well as limited participation in workplace networks serve as barriers to promotion and advancement. Additionally, women and underrepresented minorities are less likely to be assigned to key tasks and initiatives that grow experience and knowledge in emerging and

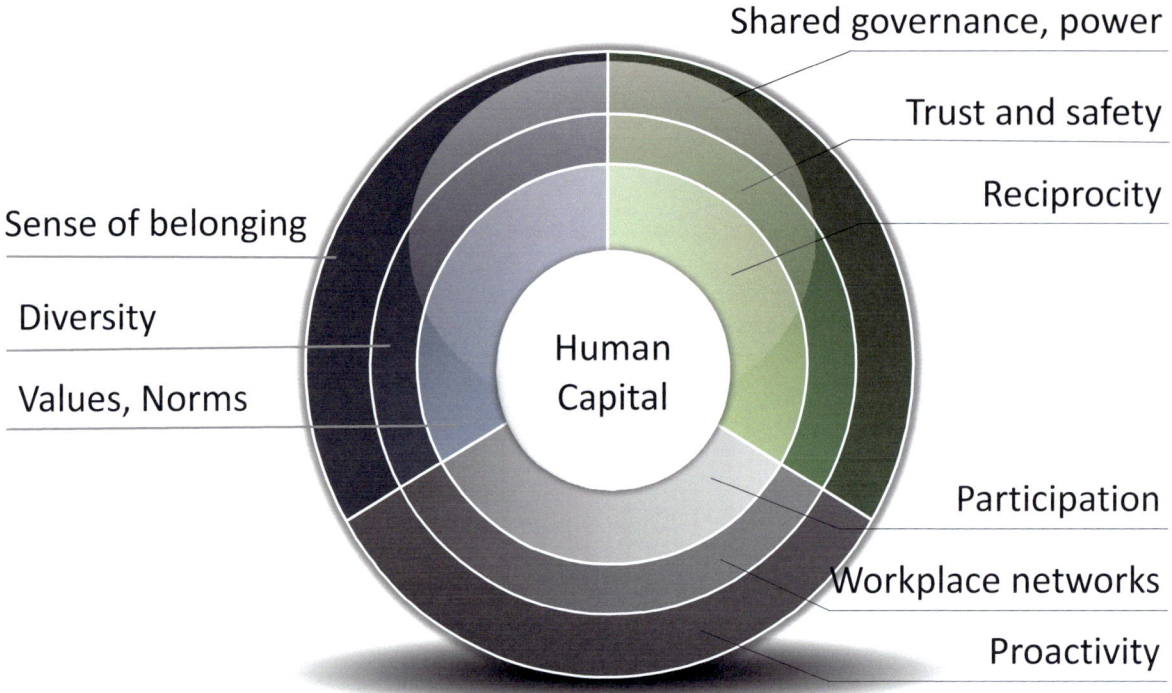

FIGURE 4-1 Human capital model of retention.
SOURCE: Committee adapted from Etti (2020).

competitive areas. Another challenge to retention and advancement is associated with unfair performance evaluations and lack of feedback.

These issues identified by Naff (1994) and others map to the Etti concepts of workplace networks, participation, proactivity, sense of belonging, and reciprocity. In the aforementioned retention barriers identified by the FAA, implementation of a human capital development process would be impactful. Particularly, if salary competition threatens retention, then proactive methods to create clear paths to advancement and higher salaries within the FAA would reduce this threat. Similarly, success at retention early in an employee's FAA career could provide opportunities to grow and develop expertise in systems thinking around cybersecurity, such that an employee may be cross-trained to understand interdependencies across all relevant components. This form of joint optimization within human capital development advances the personal growth of the employee and their readiness and productivity within the organization, each of which lead to advancements consistent with organizational values.

Focusing on Management Practices and Attitudes as Leading Indicators of Employee Intent to Depart from an Organization

To be effective, human capital development must be led by management practices that support the advancement of employees. Part of leadership development for managers should involve an understanding of the urgency to recruit and retain strong cybersecurity talent. The FAA identified an increasing challenge of balancing permanent cybersecurity employees with contractors, many of whom are former FAA employees (FAA, 2020). It is prudent to connect the dots in this case. A contributor to effective human capital development is shared governance or a perceived sense of power in the workplace. Managers play a significant role in employee perceived power (Schrage et al., 2020). Thus, management styles must be continuously assessed and developed to determine the extent to which a management style is conducive to an effective human capital development strategy.

One indicator on management performance evaluations would be a demonstrated ability to be proactive and inclusive in identifying talent in the workplace that could benefit from high levels of human capital development. In meeting its own Goal 4 in the 2020–2025 FAA Cybersecurity Strategy, the agency's employees and management are key to co-designing and implementing human capital development processes that build and maintain a competitive workforce (FAA, 2020). As mentioned, the objectives of Goal 4 included providing more cybersecurity training and experiential learning (exercises). In combination, achieving the objective of role-based training to help employees better understand their roles and how their roles fit within a larger structure was deemed important in the strategy (Goal 4 objective). Management's ability to execute this objective is another performance indicator for strong leadership in human capital development. Great managers focus on making people better at what they do.

Another practice in the development of managers and other leaders in the FAA is the capability to recognize factors that may impact turnover rates. Many studies focus on the intention to turnover (or leave) an organization, but there are fewer studies focusing on actual turnover rates. A study by Cohen, Blake, and Goodman (2016) did apply a linear regression model to identify factors that correlated with actual turnover rates. They found that workload satisfaction was strongly correlated with actual turnover rates. Higher workload and perceived unfairness in workload distribution led to more dissatisfaction and turnover. Also, lower satisfaction with advancement opportunities in the organization led to higher turnover rates. When employees saw limited opportunities to move to higher positions, they were more likely to leave for better opportunities. Not surprisingly, pay satisfaction also correlated strongly with turnover rates. The fourth contributor was flexibility in work schedules, such that more set and rigid work schedules were associated with higher turnover rates.

Advancing Workplace Culture to Enhance Attractiveness of the Organization to Recruit and Retain Employees

Although the FAA has suggested that retention is not as great a challenge as recruitment, continued challenges with recruitment amidst an existing experienced workforce may be a leading indicator of an organizational culture that may not be evolving to the degree necessary to attract and retain younger workers (FAA, 2020). Additionally, the loss of employees to private industry and other government agencies might very well signal the need for examination of organizational culture at least as a negative contributor to retention.

Organizational culture defines the proper way to behave within the organization. This culture consists of shared beliefs and values established by leaders and then communicated and reinforced through various methods, ultimately shaping employee perceptions, behaviors, and understanding.[8] Organizational culture is a key factor in the success of an organization as it can make or break any enterprise.

A study by Opengart and Ison (2016) focusing on personnel shortages in aviation collected factors from interviews of women in aviation, one of the most difficult populations to recruit and retain. Based on interviews, barriers were identified that relate to workplace practices. For example, a lack of open communication was a persistent annoyance for women in aviation, because women did not feel comfortable expressing needs that might be different from those assumed by the predominantly male leadership. This inability to openly communicate influenced decisions to leave aviation, regardless of talent, expertise, and passion for the job.

Opengart and Ison (2016) also found that fair distribution of work was another factor. Workload and fairness in workload distribution should be a value embedded in the organizational culture; one that values employees as the greatest resource. In the Opengart and Ison study, the perception of unequal distribution, either through overload or through which assignments were given to which aviation employees, was considered a contributor to dissatisfaction in the workplace. Other factors identified by women included a sense that the fight for equality in a male-dominated aviation culture was cognitively exhausting, leading to distractions in their ability to focus on critical tasks. Finally, self-efficacy was undermined by a workplace culture that valued men over women and stereotyped women as being less capable. These stereotypes may also have been reinforced through the exclusion of women in key networks and group activities. These practices, shaped by a specific organizational culture, undermine almost every concept identified in the Etti model for human capital. In essence, women who wanted higher

---

[8]More information is available at: https://www.shrm.org/resourcesandtools/tools-and-samples/toolkits/pages/understandinganddeveloping organizationalculture.aspx.

or better compensation, reported being blocked from building human capital in the aviation workplace, and, consequently, they made the decision to go elsewhere to pursue opportunities perceived to be more fair and lucrative.

As the Opengart and Ison (2016) study illustrates, retention is associated with organizational culture, and in particular, building an organization where employees perceive opportunities to develop human capital while also working within an organization that offers opportunity and flexibility. Newer generations with tendencies toward higher career mobility will not easily be retained without future-oriented best practices for retention. To avoid a revolving door and keep the best talent to meet increasingly complex and rapidly changing cybersecurity threats, a strong focus on organizational culture must be central to any organization's priorities and strategic goals. But an intentional plan and process to facilitate retention also needs to be focused on cybersecurity positions in particular.

One way to focus the effort is to conduct a barrier analysis specific to the cybersecurity workforce. This barrier analysis, in the committee's judgment should be comprehensive and should involve diverse employees, including early-career employees, women, different generations, and underrepresented minorities. There is a need to build a culture of cybersecurity across all facets of an organization. A better positioned workforce will be the first line of defense. The goal is to have workers do what you would have them do to protect systems on their own. By better training the staff on the threats and making it more competitive this will inspire some employees to pursue cyber careers. A "women in technology" program in collaboration with the Women in Technology organization[9] can help demonstrate the value and importance an organization or agency is placing on recruiting and advancing women in cybersecurity.

TALENT PIPELINE DEVELOPMENT

Addressing the gap in the cybersecurity workforce requires programs that help employers identify the required skills and education programs that develop those skills at all levels of education (i.e., early, mid, and late career). There are several programs and initiatives specifically focused on developing the cybersecurity workforces at the general education, university, and professional levels. Some initiatives are designed to develop a talented cybersecurity workforce and attract them to work in government agencies (Piotrowski, 2020).

Some of these initiatives are designed to characterize cybersecurity knowledge, skills, and abilities to improve understanding of what is required in various cybersecurity roles. The National Initiative Cybersecurity Education (NICE) Framework was developed to provide a common frame of reference and common language to describe cybersecurity roles and the knowledge, skills, and abilities needed to perform work in those roles (Newhouse et al., 2017). Mapping existing and future job roles to knowledge, skills, and job tasks like those in the NICE Framework is a crucial step in establishing a cybersecurity workforce. It is important to understand what skills are required for each job role so that recruitment and training efforts ensure the required skills in the cybersecurity workforce, and using a common framework may help standardize within different lines of business within the FAA and across organizations. It is also important to recognize that lacking current knowledge and skills in the cyber realm need not be a barrier to pursuing training or a career in cyber, as having requisite aptitudes and traits (e.g., systems thinking, need for cognition) serve as a sufficient predictor for future competency in cyber occupations (Coovert, Wiernik, and Martin, 2019, 2020).

In the committee's judgment, there may be resistance to investments in the talent pipeline because these investments are for the long term and do not fill current positions, may be viewed as a distraction, and may divert resources from other needs. However, such investments are in the national interest and in a governmental organizations' long-term interests.

Early Training Talent Pipeline Development

There has been focus in recent years on developing skills and interest in cybersecurity at the K–12 level. For example, the United States Department of Homeland Security (DHS) Cybersecurity Education Training Assistance Program (CETAP) and the Air Force Association's CyberPatriot National Youth Cyber Education Program are

---

[9]More information is available at: https://www.womenintechnology.org.

intended to give K–12 teachers cybersecurity education tools to develop an awareness of cybersecurity issues and career fields.[10] Government agencies may help ensure the long-term workforce needs are met by actively supporting and visibly participating in these programs. There are increasing efforts and studies aimed at high school students to attract future talent and increase the perceived value of cyber science (Turner et al., 2014).

The largest high school cyber defense competition is the Air Force Association's CyberPatriot competition program.[11] This program was created to inspire K–12 students toward cybersecurity or STEM careers and gives teams the task of managing a network for a small company. The competition is at the core of the program and involves middle and high school students.

Another organization making high-quality computer science an integral part of the K–12 educational experience is CSforALL.[12] The CSforALL initiative connects providers, schools, funders, and researchers to equip students with computational thinking skills.

Other programs for younger elementary (K–6) school children include the Air Force Association's CyberCamps, which teach the basics of cybersecurity, and the Cyber Education Literature series for early elementary students.[13] Other organizations have also implemented programs aimed at younger children, such as the Girl Scouts of USA's Cyber Challenge. In 2019, a national computer science program was sponsored by Raytheon to help close the gender gap in STEM fields by preparing girls to pursue careers in fields such as cybersecurity, computer science, artificial intelligence, and robotics. Finally, universities are beginning to develop programs to engage students beginning in grade school. At the University of South Florida for example, there are special coding camps targeted at several specific grade groups, including Grades 3–5 "Elementary CyberCamp"; grades 4–6 "Everyone Can Code Camp"; grades 6–8 "Middle School CyberCamp"; and grades 9–12 "High School CyberCamp."[14]

Finding 4-2: Continuing through college, groups such as the National Collegiate Cyber Defense Competition bring together highly skilled individuals about to enter the cyber workforce. Groups and activities such as these provide opportunities for an organization to contact and recruit developing cyber talent.

College-Level Talent Pipeline Development

Programs directed at training university students and recruiting them to government agencies have been successful in providing high-quality graduates of programs to federal agencies. The Scholarship for Service (SFS) program[15] is the most well-known of the internship programs for cybersecurity. SFS students receive fellowships in exchange for 2 years of service in a federal agency. As discussed in Chapter 3, the majority of employees hired through the SFS program stay in the position beyond the required service time. Because there are a limited number of SFS graduates, and graduates can choose which government agency in which to serve their required time, competition for these graduates is keen. To take full advantage of the SFS program, employers need to actively recruit SFS graduates and ensure their workplace is perceived as desirable.

The National Security Agency (NSA) and the DHS sponsor the National Centers of Academic Excellence in Cyber Defense Education (CAE-CDE) program.[16] This program aims to decrease vulnerability in the nation's infrastructure through cyber defense education and research. The program includes the CAE-CDE program for Associate, Bachelor, Masters, and Doctoral programs; and the Centers of Academic Excellence in Cyber Research (CAE-R). The CAE-CDE is a "national quality standard for certifying and maintaining high quality of cybersecurity education with rigorous and consistent requirements for program evaluation and close alignment to specific

---

[10] More information is available at: https://niccs.us-cert.gov/formal-education/integrating-cybersecurity-classroom.

[11] More information about the Air Force Association's CyberPatriot program is available at: https://www.uscyberpatriot.org/.

[12] More information about CSforALL is available at: https://www.csforall.org/.

[13] More information is available at: https://www.uscyberpatriot.org/afa-cybercamps/getting-started/afa-cybercamp-overview and https://www.uscyberpatriot.org/Pages/Special%20Initiatives/CELS-Overview.aspx

[14] More information is available at: https://www.usf.edu/education/about-us/summer-programs.aspx.

[15] More information is available at: https://www.sfs.opm.gov/.

[16] More information about the history and management of the CAE-CDE is available at: https://www.nsa.gov/resources/students-educators/centers-academic-excellence/.

cybersecurity knowledge units" (Dawson et al., 2018, p. 127). Dawson and colleagues note that "[o]ut of over 5300 colleges and universities in the U.S., only about 200 of them have achieved the CAE-CDE designation status" (p. 127).

Currently, education for cybersecurity is available at 2- and 4-year academic institutions, with varying courses, programs, and degrees. These may be focused on cybersecurity, computer science and engineering, management information systems, and other information technology-related areas (NRC, 2013). Cybersecurity education is also available as part of other fields of study such as business.

There is a current push for universities to establish centers to advance cybersecurity education and workforce development programs, such as the Virginia Tech program to help Amazon's new headquarters staffing.[17] Their roles vary, including curriculum development, co-curricular initiatives, building of the K–12 pipeline, and so forth. Another example is the Center for Infrastructure Assurance and Security (CIAS) at The University of Texas at San Antonio, which created the Collegiate Cyber Defense Competition (CCDC)[18] along with several other competition programs. CCDC is similar to other competitions in many ways; however, it is the only one that focuses on managing and protecting an existing network infrastructure. The competition, especially the top performers, routinely attracts recruiters for hiring.

Diversity Through College-Level Talent Pipeline Development

One path to increasing the talent pool available to a cyber workforce would be to emphasize the recruitment of minorities and women, groups that have traditionally been overlooked in this field (Burrell, 2018). As discussed above, programs in higher education can be an effective component of an organization's recruitment and selection strategy; this includes efforts to increase the diversity of the cyber workforce. As recently pointed out (NASEM, 2019), a great pool of potential STEM talent can be found at the more than 700 minority-serving institutions (MSIs) across the United States.

Finding 4-3: Institutional partnerships with MSIs can both expand the talent pool for high-demand positions and ensure diversity in the workforce for the long term.

Student-Level Talent Pipeline Development

Beyond institution-level initiatives to promote cybersecurity, interventions with individual students can also bolster the cybersecurity talent pipeline. Scholarship programs, such as those administered through the Center for Cyber Safety and Education (Center), formerly (ISC)² Foundation, provide scholarship opportunities for undergraduate, graduate, minorities, women, and Veterans.[19] The 2020 KnowBe4 Scholarship for Black Americans in Cybersecurity is a $10,000 scholarship that can be used for tuition, fees, books, electronics, and housing, while the 2020 (ISC)² Women's Scholarship provides $1,000 to $6,000 to individual women pursuing or planning to pursue a degree in the field of cybersecurity or information assurance.

FAA TALENT PIPELINE DEVELOPMENT

There are well-established models for MSI student internships at other federal agencies that the FAA might consider adopting or adapting. The National Geospatial-Intelligence Agency and NSA are good examples. In the committee's judgment, the most effective internship programs are centered around the student experience, such as supporting mentorship and other engagement with students throughout the academic year.

A spectrum of opportunities for broader engagement exists that runs from informal interactions with faculty to support for campus visits by FAA employees, and providing support for scholars-in-residence. Such activi-

---

[17] More information is available at: https://vt.edu/innovationcampus/News/2019/June/innovation-campus-location.html.
[18] More information on competition details is available at: https://www.nationalccdc.org/.
[19] More information about all the scholarship opportunities is available at: https://iamcybersafe.org/s/scholarships.

ties would represent a change in practice and culture from what the committee understands to be the norm in cybersecurity at the FAA. The FAA does this in other areas of the organization, and both NSA and CIA support scholars-in-residence programs at MSIs for this purpose. FAA technical staff and managers can both proactively reach out to faculty and use research with universities as an opportunity to develop relationships with faculty who will create talent pipelines.

There may be a need to create new programs to meet unique or specific FAA cyber workforce needs. For example, there may not currently be education and training programs targeted at detailed government technical oversight of industry technical programs (i.e., aircraft manufacturers).

To formalize a human-centric cyber-education curriculum, Caulkins and colleagues (2016) analyzed the NICE, the National Cybersecurity Workforce Framework, and the DHS National Initiative for Cybersecurity Careers and Studies (NICCS) educational framework. After a gap-analysis, the human-centric educational training curriculum was developed and implemented in a pilot educational program at a large university. Important elements of this work include the integration of three overarching frameworks, a gap analysis, and the focus on human-centric training for behavioral cybersecurity.

How might we conceptualize training for a cybersecurity workforce? And how might these be applied to the FAA's situation in particular? One proposed model is to utilize a framework associated with military strategy (Church, 2016). There are several flavors proposed, but the author argues that we can leverage what we do well in the military and apply it as a framework for dealing with cyber issues. Another strategy often advocated is that the focus of cyber awareness training should be to try to "get into the attacker's head." Many training programs to thwart attackers focus only on the explicit—that which is observable. Martiny and colleagues (2015) believe a more successful approach would be to try and understand the belief states and goals of the attacker. This argues for training a cognitive understanding of the attacker.

Training

Training is an essential part of a cyber aware workforce. Key elements include training regarding social engineering and that the fact any part of the cyber-physical system can be attacked. Developments in the training area include the fact that individuals with different personality factors are more or less likely to succumb to threats of social engineering (Cusack and Adedokun, 2018; SEI, 2014). Cloud-based training has developed the capability of providing training at both the worksite and off worksite of the employee. Additionally, developments of training strategies employing serious games, gamification, and digital sandboxes of different types are increasing the capability to provide realistic training under realistic conditions for a variety of cyber-related occupations.

Formal training methods are employed by the FAA where individuals are sent to universities for specialized cyber training for short periods.[20] Other less formal training approaches include peer mentoring (Janeja et al., 2016) and peer influence (Li et al., 2016b) to improve cybersecurity behavior in organizations. Zafar (2016) advocates for the use of behavioral training, having found correlations between habit creation and security threats (e.g., password sharing, phishing, unauthorized cloud computing).

Below are three examples of what the committee means by personnel practices that could support professional development and motivate the cyber workforce. These are not intended as mandates, but illustrations of policies and procedures that likely would benefit the FAA.

1. Allow time away and expensing of registration fees for security workshops.
2. Strategically and fairly use temporary duty assignments to other agencies or FFRDCs so that staff can assess and import security practices that have proven to work well elsewhere.
3. Make broader use of, and publicize internally, short-term "red teams" that allow security-minded technical staff, even those without NICE security job titles, to research new attack techniques on FAA systems,

---

[20]Focus group discussion with FAA employees and committee members, August 20, 2020. All discussions were conducted in confidentiality, and the names of the participants are withheld by mutual agreement. Focus group discussion with FAA managers and committee members, August 21, 2020.

whether in Atlantic City test facilities or elsewhere. Perhaps more important than the budget outlay is the management skill in creating "blameless post-mortems" (i.e., after action reviews of lessons learned) that widely spread the knowledge gained through the FAA without creating embarrassment or hard feelings.

Skill Development and Training Through Certification

Along with formalized academic training, certification programs can be used to complement and expand cybersecurity knowledge, skills, and abilities. Organizations providing certifications have the advantage of frequently updating information and competencies while also being more responsive to emerging threats in the cybersecurity landscape (Knapp et al., 2017). Other programs such as the U.S. Cyber Challenge (USCC) have identified strategies to train and assess students to fulfill cybersecurity roles.

Workplace Flexibility

Workplace flexibility is a powerful tool to apply in retention as well as recruiting (as discussed in Chapter 3). Changes in telecommuting perspectives related to the COVID-19 pandemic are becoming increasingly cited as an important issue for employees. Work-life balance is an important factor for many younger employees and is increasingly important for all employees (Singh, 2019). Flexible work schedules and flexibility in work location may be a way to bring talent to less desirable locations. Organizations having difficulty retraining or keeping employees because of the work locations should consider allowing telecommuting for job roles that do not require employees to be on site.

RETIREMENT

As discussed in Chapter 2 of this report, the FAA has an experienced workforce with many employees getting closer to retirement-eligible age or having accumulated the years necessary to retire from the organization. For years, experts have been predicting a wave of retirements in the federal government, and urging federal agencies to prepare for the inevitable "tsunami" of retirement-eligible employees leaving the workforce (Lewis and Cho, 2011). This anticipated shift has prompted focus on how to recruit and retain the numbers needed to maintain the workforce and how to capture knowledge from these highly skilled employees. In its interviews, the committee heard about employees staying on past their retirement because they enjoy the mission and experience a sense of fulfillment working in their current positions, but this is not a long-term or comprehensive solution. It is critical that an organization develop strategies to ensure that specialized knowledge related to its mission and operation is captured and transferred effectively to new employees. One strategy would be to establish a list of critical positions within the cybersecurity workforce and track the succession plans for each position on a regular basis.

Such a large wave of retirements also presents any organization with an opportunity to identify shifts in the needed skills and knowledge and recruit employees to fill gaps. The fast pace of changes in cybersecurity affects the skills and knowledge needed to effectively perform cybersecurity, which means that job functions may change equally rapidly (Vasileiou and Furnell, 2019). On-the-job training and reskilling can support the development of these skills but in limited ways, and some job functions may require recruiting new individuals with unique skillsets and experiences (Burrell, 2018). Taking advantage of openings due to retirements may allow the opportunity to evaluate emergent needs and refresh the workforce with those new skills (Dawson and Thomson, 2018). As workers retire, it is important for managers and recruiters to avoid replicating the position description of the outgoing employee and rushing to hire workers with identical skillsets. Instead, they might take the time to look at where the cybersecurity workforce is moving and recast the position for the future, critically evaluating what new skills might be required. Though this takes additional time, it is likely well worth the effort to thoroughly understand present organizational needs, project future needs, and how to further the diversity of skills through a conceptualization of these positions. This may be an effective strategy particularly for agencies that tend to have low turnover and fewer open cybersecurity positions, such as the FAA.

CYBERSECURITY ORGANIZATIONAL STRUCTURE AND DESIGN

Organizational design is a strategic management approach that considers people, system complexity, and organizational aspirations. Other factors such as emerging behaviors and needs, core business priorities, geopolitical requirements, and the external environment are also considered (Auernhammer and Leifer, 2019; Hendrick, 2009). Part of any business strategy that impacts organizational design relates to the use of assets and tools to advance the goals of the organization (Moşteanu, 2020). Tagarev (2020) has identified important considerations for organizational design in collaborative cybersecurity organizations; these include a governance structure within the overall organization design with a focus on trust, security risk, knowledge sharing, and inter-operability. While there are numerous models for structuring an organization, including hierarchical, matrixed, and functional structures and others, the distributed nature and breadth of missions at the FAA has resulted in an organization that incorporates aspects of each of these.

The FAA cybersecurity workforce alignment presently supports two functional areas, the enterprise role and the mission systems. The enterprise role includes support of the internal infrastructure and processes, cyber operations, security awareness training and application, and network enterprise services. Mission functions encompass the air traffic systems, unmanned systems, other platforms, and system of systems to support the FAA missions. The mission-facing cybersecurity workforce performs acquisition duties as well as design, testing, and oversight for specific programs. In the committee's judgment, organizations benefit from including organizational design as a part of continuous improvement to ensure that the structure and processes are optimized to align the workforce with the mission.

In the committee's judgment, organizational design is not simply an effort to assert functional and cross-functional capabilities, but also a means of communicating the values of an organization and its outward-facing commitment to the mission (it should be noted this could be tied to how the FAA markets itself). Training and communication are important aspects of the human-centered approach and are enabled by both organizational structure and culture. These aspects of organizational design have become an industry best practice, as discussed in relation to the United Postal Service (UPS) (Perez, 2020) and summarized in McKinsey & Company research (Lewis, 2020).

Further information-gathering briefings during this study provided more information relevant to organizational design and the success of the FAA cybersecurity workforce initiative. According to Juan Perez, UPS Chief Information and Engineering Officer, organizational design should establish a solid network with the appropriate technologies, the right people, the right attitude, and the appropriate planning to be able to manage events (Perez, 2020). The right people and leadership have to be in place to protect the privacy and security of a company's information (Perez, 2020). Additionally, the design of a cybersecurity organization should also be a reflection of the cybersecurity risk management governance model that the organization wants to have in place.

From Perez's perspective, UPS Chief Information Officers (CIOs) and Chief Information Security Officers (CISOs) must have six capabilities concerning cybersecurity:

1. Know the company;
2. Know the customer;
3. Understand security and information breaches;
4. Prioritize what is most critical and important to protect;
5. Establish a well-defined response mechanism to any potential incident; and
6. Apply these capabilities consistently.

According to Perez, cybersecurity requires collective efforts. Similar to Hendrick (2009), Perez observed that the complexity of the system will influence the effectiveness of organizational design and the capabilities of those assigned in leadership roles in specific organizational units. In the committee's judgement, simplifying the complexity of the system through technology, automation, and better processes and controls is critical.

The FAA cybersecurity workforce efforts will benefit from best practices, such as those forged by UPS and similar organizations, which include a people-centric perspective on the workforce. UPS focuses on socializing employees to facilitate a security-minded enterprise, and this socialization is done through teaching, training, standardizing risk management, and communicating to foster a security culture and individual awareness (Perez,

2020). Agility is a critical benefit of this people-centric perspective. Based on organizational theory, too much centralization may restrict the agility of an organization, especially those that rely on knowledge-based roles (as opposed to routinized or skill-based roles) (Hendrick, 2009; Moşteanu, 2020).

Charlie Lewis, Expert Associate Partner at McKinsey & Company, provided information on organizational design from the perspective of strategic management. Trends in how organizations are changing include challenges with organizational leadership, talent acquisition and retention, risk-based investment, business enablement, cyber hygiene, and regulatory compliance. According to Lewis, when thinking about how an organization should be structured, organizational leadership needs to be empowered to influence the business. CISO units should not be perceived as a wall or impediment. They should be seen as innovation enablers.

It is important for cybersecurity in any organization to fit within the structure and the operating model of the broader business and to be a part of the broader business or the broader organization in a way that allows it to support the achievement of the business strategic goals and understand what to secure, why to secure, and where their focus should be in both how they operate to support delivering value and determining the competencies needed (Lewis, 2020). Additionally, the processes, integration, and linkages required with existing governance structures need to be considered across the entire business. Finally, in thinking about how to structure the organization, Lewis suggested bringing in new people, and take the processes and the operating models decided upon to structure the organization as a whole (Lewis, 2020).

Lewis explained that when looking at the operating model as a cyber-specific operating model, there are key design choices to consider. These design choices include the service catalog (what are the services provided and where do they go), risk ownership (clarifying the division of stakeholders who are accountable, responsible, consulted, and/or informed in the cyber risk management process), and lines of defense (as they pertain to cybersecurity and risk are discussed in more detail below). In his presentation, Lewis outlined three lines of defense for cybersecurity:

- The first line typically includes the IS department and business units.
- The second line of defense is composed of risk managers looking at aggregate risks at an enterprise level.
- The third line evaluates the overall process of cyber risk governance.[21]

For the most part, these are fairly standard operating model design considerations that would be applied. Cybersecurity should be no different from any other part of the organization. It just serves a different, newer function. Close coordination across these three independent lines of defense is enabled by five foundational elements that are the keys to success: (1) lifecycle understanding of controls; (2) strong process definition; (3) clear definition of roles and responsibilities; (4) talent distribution; and (5) enterprise-wide agreement between roles and responsibilities (Lewis, 2020). The key takeaway is that there should be close coordination across these independent lines. They may be independent, but they need to work together.

Peter Cooper, CEO of Pavisade, discussed cybersecurity challenges in the aviation workforce. Leadership coordination, accountability, and expertise in aerospace safety are fairly well understood throughout the entire organization in aerospace, all the way up to the CEO (Cooper, 2020). For example, there are dedicated flight safety chains and a well-established culture of flight safety. But for aviation and aerospace cybersecurity, the challenge is finding the balance between leadership, coordination, accountability, and expertise.

Cooper noted it is critical to understand workforce push and pull factors to attract, develop, and retain a cybersecurity workforce. The future workforce will need to:

"develop new regulations; understand complex cyber/physical systems at the edge of innovation; understand complex failure modes and resiliency; have the confidence to question and challenge; have the ability to objectively test/audit and demonstrate; and to make and communicate, objective, evidential, risk-based decisions; and defend those decisions" (Cooper, 2020).

---

[21] More information is available at: https://securityintelligence.com/take-a-load-off-delegate-cyber-risk-management-using-the-three-lines-of-defense-model/.

The CISO as a Senior Executive

Given the critical nature of cybersecurity to the FAA's mission, the reporting lines for the CISO need to respect the role as senior within the organization. Every operational and technology decision carries risks to the cyber enterprise and can impact FAA operations and thus impact flight safety. In the committee's judgement, to manage the risk appropriately, the CISO must be included, irrespective of human resource reporting structures.

To better illustrate the degree to which the significance of the CISO role has been elevated in the private sector, the committee points to the National Association of Corporate Directors (NACD) and Internet Security Alliance, who made clear "directors need to understand and approach cybersecurity as a strategic, enterprise risk—not just as an IT risk" (Clinton et al., 2020, p. 12). As a result, the NACD suggests that Boards of Directors build a personal relationship with their CISOs. From the discussions with various presenters the committee found that the most effective CISOs operate at multiple levels and believe it is important for the FAA's CISO to be able to develop a comprehensive cybersecurity strategy that crosses multiple complex domains.

Given the highly complex nature of the FAA and the potential for life-threatening cyber events, the FAA needs to build plans around recruitment, development, and retention of highly skilled, knowledgeable, and innovative CISOs.

Finding 4-4: The FAA cybersecurity employees and the cybersecurity program as a whole will benefit from a CISO that can develop a comprehensive cybersecurity strategy that crosses multiple complex domains in the FAA.

CISO Independence

In the committee's judgment, it is critical that the CISO have a high degree of independence in order to challenge failures to execute key security controls. The most common historical failures have resulted from CISOs reporting to CIOs. This often creates conflicts of interest in areas such as vulnerability and patch management, technology choices, and outsourcing decisions. The emerging best practice in many private-sector organizations that have had CISOs reporting to CIOs has been to elevate the role to become a peer of the CIO. In some cases, this also involves expanding the typical scope of the CISO to include other risk disciplines, most frequently business continuity and technology resilience. In the private sector, another best practice is to allow the CISO to have direct access to the Board of Directors.

Three Lines of Defense

In the financial services industry, an emerging best practice in cyberecurity risk management is the idea of multiple lines of defense. These are:

1. The business and the IS operational teams that own the risks and execute the security program;
2. An independent function to challenge the appropriateness of risk management decisions; and
3. An audit or control validation function.

The three-lines-of-defense model originated in banking and was focused on credit risk, market risk, and counter-party risk. In the early 2010s, banking regulators began to extend the concept to operational risk, most visibly cybersecurity risk. In 2013, the Institute of Internal Auditors published a position paper, "The Three Lines of Defense in Effective Risk Management and Control," that introduced and extended the best practice outside of banking to other large enterprises (IIA, 2013).

In an organization, the CISO is the functional leader for the first line of defense, and the Inspector General is the functional leader for the third line of defense. There is no leader of the second line today. The role of the second line is not to create a second audit organization. While auditors need to be focused on the controls and whether or not they are being operated effectively, the new second line is not "controls" focused. The second line's role is at a higher level and includes examining the risk management decisions being made and, when necessary, questioning whether those decisions will force the organization to operate outside of its risk tolerances.

Hybrid/Federate First Line CISO Teams

Based on private-sector best practices, neither a fully centralized nor a fully decentralized model for a first-line cybersecurity program can be effective in a large complex organization. To best deliver on the mission, the cybersecurity organization itself is ideally, in the committee's judgement, a hybrid organization composed of two basic types of teams: (1) a cybersecurity organization-wide team and (2) a vertically integrated specialized team.

Ideally, one core set of teams would support the entire FAA in a shared and horizontally integrated fashion. These teams would directly report to the FAA's CISO, and their budgets, in the committee's judgement, should be centrally managed. These teams would focus on governance functions as well as the development and operations of critical capabilities that need to operate across the enterprise to be operationally and economically effective.

These core teams would be augmented by a set of highly specialized teams that are vertically integrated with the different units they support within the FAA ecosystem even as they remain connected to the core. These teams could be matrix managed by both the CISO as well as the lead role of the group with which they are aligned. The budget for these groups should be managed by the CISO as agreed with the relevant department heads.

The key first line horizontal functions are:[22]

- Strategy and governance
  - Policy writing
  - Cyber tech strategy
  - Risk measurement and reporting
  - Risk identification/risk acceptance or policy exception management
- Information security operations
  - Identity and access management
  - Vulnerability and threat management inclusive of red team
  - Data protection
  - Supply-chain IS risk management
- Cybersecurity operations
  - Security operations center
  - Threat hunting
  - Incident response
  - Cyber threat intelligence
  - Cybersecurity fusion center
- Core security technology engineering and architecture standards
  - Network, data center, cloud, and end point security engineering
  - Application security architecture and engineering
  - Cyber innovation

As the first-line security engineering and operations teams are built, another private-sector best practice should be, in the committee's judgment, overlaid on the previous model; this is the idea of organizing around the concept of Plan, Build, and Operate (PBO). Under the PBO rubric, one function would excel at strategy, one at engineering, and one at execution, with all tied together through the shared services delivery goal.

Examples of vertical/local functions are:

- FAA Internal Applications Security Specialists;
- FAA External Applications Security Specialists;

---

[22]This is meant to be an illustration of one such model; many variations will exist.

- FAA External Airframe Security Specialists; and
- FAA Airport Security Specialists.

Concluding Thoughts on Organizational Structure and Design

In the above sections, best practices associated with organizational design have been enumerated along with examples. Given the changing demographics of the United States, best practices, in the committee's judgement, would ideally align with future cybersecurity needs and would include the populations that have not been equitably considered as contributors of their talent, skills, and knowledge to the FAA. Intentional efforts to apply these workforce best practices are integral to recruiting, developing, and retaining a robust cybersecurity workforce.

SUMMARY

This chapter has examined how the FAA should retain the talent needed for a diverse cybersecurity organization. Using the ELC model as guidance, the committee has made findings and recommendations in the areas of retention, development and advancement, and retirement. At every point, the committee has also considered issues of diversity. With these as a path forward, the committee believes that the FAA will be able to over time become a high-performing and diverse cybersecurity organization.

Conclusions and Recommendations

Difficulty competing with commercial entities that have higher compensation packages is one of the current challenges faced by the FAA in building its cybersecurity workforce. While one of the biggest benefits of working in the private sector is the higher salary potential, organizational reputation and positioning are critical components of recruitment and talent attraction efforts. The FAA relies on its staff to be mission focused and supports their cybersecurity workforce to complete their tasks.

As described in Chapter 3, managing an employee's success and thus the organization's success, takes place across multiple stages: attraction, recruitment and hiring (onboarding), development, advancement, retention, and retirement (separation). These are critical components that the FAA can and should pursue as indicated in the recommendations below.

CONCLUSION 4-1: It is critical that the Federal Aviation Administration develop strategies to ensure that specialized knowledge related to the FAA mission and operation is captured and transferred effectively to new employees.

RECOMMENDATION 4-1: The Federal Aviation Administration should monitor, and revise if necessary, its personnel practices to support the development of the necessary skills to meet the ever-changing demand in the current and future cybersecurity workforce.

RECOMMENDATION 4-2: The Federal Aviation Administration should provide professional development opportunities to refresh skill sets of current cybersecurity employees and ensure sharing of key institutional and mission-specific knowledge with newer cybersecurity staff.

RECOMMENDATION 4-3: The Federal Aviation Administration (FAA) cybersecurity employees and the cybersecurity program as a whole will benefit from a Chief Information Security Officer (CISO) that can develop a comprehensive cybersecurity strategy that crosses multiple complex domains in the FAA. The CISO's reporting structure needs to support a strong governance model, which ensures that the CISO has both the independence and the access required to effectively manage the FAA's cyber risk posture. In support of such leadership responsibility, the FAA should position the CISO role at the most senior level of the non-political appointees within the organization. Given the scarcity of qualified

people, the FAA should consider variances from current pay-scale limitations in order to be a competitive employer.

RECOMMENDATION 4-4: Employee retirement, at the end of the lifecycle model, offers organizations the opportunity to rethink organizational needs and required skill sets, which in turn helps refocus talent recruitment and the next iteration of the employee lifecycle. The Federal Aviation Administration should ensure that all efforts to upskill and evolve the cyber workforce include the agency's risk management, cybersecurity compliance, and independent assurance capabilities.

RECOMMENDATION 4-5: The Federal Aviation Administration should enable the success of the cybersecurity program and the Chief Information Security Officer by designing a hybrid organizational model leveraging private-sector best practices such as blending core and edge (vertically integrated) functions as well as the plan, build, operate model.

REFERENCES

Abdullah, N., Shonubi, O.A., Hashim, R., and Hamid, N. 2016. Recognition and appreciation and its psychological effect on job satisfaction and performance in a Malaysia IT company: systematic review. *IOSR Journal of Humanities and Social Science*, 21(9), 47–55.

Allen, D.G., Bryant, P.C., and Vardaman, J.M. 2010. Retaining talent: Replacing misconceptions with evidence-based strategies. *Academy of Management Perspectives*, 48–64.

Alnachef, T., and Alhajjar, A. 2015. Effect of human capital on organizational performance: A literature review. *International Journal of Science and Research, 6*, 1154–1158.

Auernhammer, J.M.K., and Leifer, L. 2019. Is Organizational Design a Human-Centered Design Practice? *Proceedings of the 22nd International Conference on Engineering Design (ICED19)*, Delft, The Netherlands. doi: 10.1017/dsi.2019.126.

Borman, W.C., Hanson, M.A., and Hedge, J.W. 1997. Personnel selection. *Annual Review of Psychology*, 48(1), 299–337.

Bourdieu, P. 1989. Social space and symbolic power. *Sociological Theory, 7*, 14–15.

Burrell, D.N. 2018. An exploration of the cybersecurity workforce shortage. *International Journal of Hyperconnectivity and the Internet of Things*, 2(1), 29–41. doi: 10.4018/IJHIoT.2018010103.

Caulkins, B.D., Badillo-Urquiola, K., Bockelman, P., and Leis, R. 2016. Cyber Workforce Development Using a Behavioral Cybersecurity Paradigm. *2016 International Conference on Cyber Conflict (CyCon U.S.)*, Washington, DC, pp. 1–6, doi: 10.1109/CYCONUS.2016.7836614.

Church, A. 2016. Military Strategy as a Guide for Cybersecurity. *Proceedings of the 15th European Conference on Cyber Warfare and Security (ECCWS 2016)*, Munich, Germany, p. 58.

Clinton, L., Higgins, J., and van der Oord, F. 2020. *Cyber-Risk Oversight 2020: Key Principles and Practical Guidance for Corporate Boards*. National Association of Corporate Directors and the Internet Security Alliance. Available: https://www.casede.org/index.php/biblioteca-casede-2-0/seguridad/ciberseguridad/537-cyber-risk-oversight-2020/file.

Cohen, G., Blake, R., and Goodman, D. 2016. Does turnover intention matter? Evaluating the usefulness of turnover intention rate as a predictor of actual turnover rate. *Review of Public Personnel Administration, 36*, 240–263.

Coleman, J.S. 1988. Social capital in the creation of human capital. *American Journal of Sociology, 94*, 95–120.

Cooper, P. 2020. "Cybersecurity Challenges in Aviation – Workforce." Presentation to Committee on Cybersecurity Workforce of the Federal Aviation Administration. April 22, 2020. Virtual meeting.

Coovert, M.D., Wiernik, B., and Martin, J. 2019. *Use of Technology-Enhanced Simulations for Cyber Aptitude Assessment*. Technical Report. Plant City, FL: MDC & Associates.

Coovert, M.D., Wiernik, B., and Martin, J. 2020. *Use of Technology-Enhanced Simulations for Cyber Aptitude Assessment: Phase II Prototype Development*. Technical Report, Accession Number: AD1107016. Fort Belvoir, VA: Defense Technical Information Center.

Cross, R. and Cummings, J.N. 2004. Ties and network correlates of individual performance in knowledge-intensive work. *Academy of Management Journal, 47*, 928–937.

Cusack, B., and Adedokun, K. 2018. The impact of personality traits on user's susceptibility to social engineering attacks. In proceedings of the 16th Australian Information Security Management Conference (pp. 83-89). Perth, Australia: Edith Cowan University. Available: https://ro.ecu.edu.au/ism/228.

Cynet. 2020. *2020 Cybersecurity Salary Survey Results*. Available: https://go.cynet.com/hubfs/2020-Salary-Survey-Report.pdf.

Dawson, J., and Thomson, R. 2018. The future cybersecurity workforce: Going beyond technical skills for successful cyber performance. *Frontiers in Psychology, 9*, 744. doi: 10.3389/fpsyg.2018.00744.

Dawson M., Wang P., and Williams, K. 2018. The Role of CAE-CDE in Cybersecurity Education for Workforce Development. Pp. 127–132 in *Information Technology—New Generations*. Part of Advances in Intelligent Systems and Computing, vol. 738 (S. Latifi, ed.). Cham, Switzerland: Springer. doi: 10.1007/978-3-319-77028-4_20.

Embry, J. 2020. "U.S. Coast Guard." Presentation to Committee on Cybersecurity Workforce of the Federal Aviation Administration. June 29, 2020. Virtual meeting.

Etti, W.H.M. 2020. *A case study of women and ethnic minority manager leadership advancement in general schedule 13-15 pay scale within the U.S. Federal Civil Services*. Dissertation: University of Maryland – Eastern Shore. Proquest: 28002115.

FAA (Federal Aviation Administration). 2020. "The FAA Cybersecurity Workforce Overview." Presentation to Committee on Cybersecurity Workforce of the Federal Aviation Administration by FAA Cybersecurity Steering Committee (CSC) and FAA AHR Representatives. February 19, 2020. Washington, DC.

Fagley, N S. 2016. The Construct of Appreciation: It is So Much More Than Gratitude. Pp. 70–84 in *Perspectives on Gratitude: An Interdisciplinary Approach* (D. Carr, ed.). New York: Routledge.

Fagley, N.S. 2012. Appreciation uniquely predicts life satisfaction above demographics, the Big 5 personality factors, and gratitude. *Personality and individual Differences*, *53*(1), 59–63.

Fagley, N.S., and Adler, M.G. 2012. Appreciation: A spiritual path to finding value and meaning in the workplace. *Journal of Management, Spirituality & Religion*, *9*(2), 167–187.

Granovetter, M.S. 1973. The strength of weak ties. *American Journal of Sociology, 78,* 1360–1380.

Greenfield, G. 2020. "Building an Evidence-Based Diversity and Inclusion Strategy." Presentation to Committee on Cybersecurity Workforce of the Federal Aviation Administration. June 29, 2020.Virtual meeting.

Hendrick, H.W. 2009. A Sociotechnical Systems Model of Organizational Complexity and Design and Its Relation to Employee Cognitive Complexity. In *Proceedings of the Human Factors and Ergonomics Society 53rd Annual Meeting*, San Antonio, TX, pp. 1028–1032.

Hom, P.W., Caranikas-Walker, F., Prussia, G.E., and Griffeth, R.W. 1992. A meta-analytical structural equations analysis of a model of employee turnover. *Journal of Applied Psychology*, *77*(6), 890.

IIA (Institute of Internal Auditors). 2013. *IIA Position Paper: The Three Lines of Defense in Effective Risk Management and Control*. Available: https://na.theiia.org/standards-guidance/Public%20Documents/PP%20The%20Three%20Lines%20 of%20Defense%20in%20Effective%20Risk%20Management%20and%20Control.pdf.

Janeja, V.P., Seaman, C., Kephart, K., Gangopadhyay, A., and Everhart, A. 2016. Cybersecurity Workforce Development: A Peer Mentoring Approach. *2016 IEEE Conference on Intelligence and Security Informatics (ISI)*, pp. 267–272, doi: 10.1109/ISI.2016.7745487.

Knapp, K.J., Maurer, C., and Planchkinova, M. 2017. Maintaining a cybersecurity curriculum: Professional certifications as valuable guidance. *Journal of Information Systems Education, 28*(2), 101–14.

Krumm, S., and Hertel, G. 2013. Knowledge, Skills, Abilities and Other Characteristics (KSAOs) for Virtual Teamwork. pp. 80–99. *The Psychology of Digital Media at Work*. Psychology Press.

Lee, T.W., Hom, P., Eberly, M., and Li, J. 2018. Managing employee retention and turnover with 21st century ideas. *Organizational Dynamics, 47*(2), 88–98.

Lee, T.W., and Mitchell, T.R. 2003. Control turnover by understanding its causes. *The Blackwell Handbook of Principles of Organizational Behaviour*, 93–107.

Lee, T.W., and Mitchell, T.R. 1994. An alternative approach: The unfolding model of voluntary employee turnover. *Academy of Management Review, 19*(1), 51–89.

Levy, J.J., Richardson, J.D., Lounsbury, J.W., Stewart, D., Gibson, L.W., and Drost, A.W. 2011. Personality traits and career satisfaction of accounting professionals. *Individual Differences Research*, *9*(4).

Lewis, C. 2020. "Designing Business and Cybersecurity Strategy into Cybersecurity Operating and Organizational Models." Presentation to Committee on Cybersecurity Workforce of the Federal Aviation Administration. July 30, 2020. Virtual meeting.

Lewis, G.B., and Cho, Y.J. 2011. The aging of the state government workforce: Trends and implications. *The American Review of Public Administration, 41*(1), 48–60. doi: 10.1177/0275074009359308.

Li, J.J., Lee, T.W., Mitchell, T.R., Hom, P.W., and Griffeth, R.W. 2016a. The effects of proximal withdrawal states on job attitudes, job searching, intent to leave, and employee turnover. *Journal of Applied Psychology*, *101*(10), 1436.

Li, L., Xu, L., He, W., Chen, Y., and Chen, H. 2016b. Cyber Security Awareness and Its Impact on Employee's Behavior. *International Conference on Research and Practical Issues of Enterprise Information Systems*, Vienna, Austria, pp. 103–111. Lecture Notes in Business Information Processing, vol. 268. doi: 10.1007/978-3-319-49944-4_8.

Martiny, K., Motzek, A., and Möller, R., 2015. Formalizing Agents' Beliefs for Cybersecurity Defense Strategy Planning. *Computational Intelligence in Security for Information Systems Conference*, Burgos, Spain, pp. 15–25.

Mobley, W.H. 1977. Intermediate linkages in the relationship between job satisfaction and employee turnover. *Journal of Applied Psychology, 62*(2), 237–240. doi: 10.1037/0021-9010.62.2.237.

Moşteanu, N.R. 2020. Challenges for organizational structure and design as a result of digitalization and cybersecurity. *The Business & Management Review, 11*(1), 278–286.

Muntz, J., and Dormann, C. 2020. Moderating effects of appreciation on relationships between illegitimate tasks and intrinsic motivation: A two-wave shortitudinal study. *European Journal of Work and Organizational Psychology, 29*(3), 391–404.

Naff, K. 1994. Through the glass ceiling: Advancement of women in federal civil service. *Public Administration Review, 54*, 507–514.

Narayanan, A., Rajithakumar, S., and Menon, M. 2019. Talent management and employee retention: An integrative research framework. *Human Resource Development Review, 18*(2), 228–247.

NASEM. (National Academies of Sciences, Engineering, and Medicine). 2018. *Assessing and Responding to the Computer Science Undergraduate Enrollments*. Washington, DC: The National Academies Press.

NASEM. 2019. *Minority Serving Institutions: America's Underutilized Resource for Strengthening the STEM Workforce*. Washington, DC: The National Academies Press.

Newhouse, W. Keith, S., Scribner, B., and Witte, G. 2017. *National Initiative for Cybersecurity Education (NICE) Cybersecurity Workforce Framework*. NIST Special Publication 800-181. Gaithersburg, MD: National Institute of Standards and Technology. doi: 10.6028/NIST.SP.800-181.

NRC (National Research Council). 2013. *Professionalizing the Nation's Cybersecurity Workforce? Criteria for Decision-Making*. Washington, DC: The National Academies Press.

Opengart, R., and Ison, D. 2016. A strategy for alleviating aviation shortages through recruitment of women. *International Journal of Aviation Management, 3*, 200–219.

Perez, J. 2020. "UPS Cybersecurity Defense In-Depth Strategy." Presentation to Committee on Cybersecurity Workforce of the Federal Aviation Administration. June 29, 2020. Virtual meeting.

Pfister, I.B., Jacobshagen, N., Kälin, W., and Semmer, N.K. 2020. How does appreciation lead to higher job satisfaction? *Journal of Managerial Psychology, 25*(6), 465–479.

Piotrowski, V. 2020. "CyberCorps® Scholarship for Service Program (SFS)." Presentation to Committee on Cybersecurity Workforce of the Federal Aviation Administration. April 22, 2020. Virtual meeting.

Schrage, M., Schwartz, M., Jones, R., Kiron, D., and Buckley, N. 2020. Opportunity marketplaces: Aligning workforce investment and value creation in the enterprise. *Deloitte Insights*. April, 28, 2020. Available at: https://www2.deloitte.com/us/en/insights/focus/technology-and-the-future-of-work/importance-of-investing-in-employees.html.

Schweyer, A. 2004. *Talent Management Systems: Best Practices in Technology Solutions for Recruitment, Retention and Workforce Planning*. Toronto: John Wiley & Sons Canada, Ltd.

SEI (Software Engineering Institute). 2014. *Unintentional Insider Threats: Social Engineering*. The CERT® Insider Threat Center, Carnegie Mellon University. Available: https://resources.sei.cmu.edu/asset_files/TechnicalNote/2014_004_001_77459.pdf.

SHRM (Society for Human Resource Management). 2018. *Using Recognition and Other Workplace Efforts to Engage Employees: SHRM Survey Findings*. Available: https://www.shrm.org/hr-today/trends-and-forecasting/research-and-surveys/Pages/employee-recognition-2018.aspx.

Singh, D. 2019. A literature review on employee retention with focus on recent trends. *International Journal of Scientific Research in Science and Technology, 6*(1), 425–431.

Subramony, M. 2009. A meta-analytic investigation of the relationship between HRM bundles and firm performance. *Human Resource Management, 48*(5), 745–768.

Tagarev, T., 2020. Towards the design of a collaborative cybersecurity networked organisation: Identification and prioritisation of governance needs and objectives. *Future Internet, 12*(4), 62. doi: 10.3390/fi12040062.

Turner, G.E., Deemer, E.D., Tims, H.E., Corbett, K., and Mhire, J. 2014. Cyber value and interest development: Assessment of a STEM career intervention for high school students. *Electronic Journal of Science Education, 18*(1), 1–15.

Vasileiou, I., and Furnell, S. 2019. *Cybersecurity Education for Awareness and Compliance*. Hershey, PA: IGI Global. doi: 10.4018/978-1-5225-7847-5.

Wolfson, M.A., and Mathieu, J.E. 2018. Sprinting to the finish: Toward a theory of human capital resource complementarity. *Journal of Applied Psychology, 103*(11), 1165.

Zafar, H. 2016. Cybersecurity: Role of Behavioral Training in Healthcare. *Twenty-second Americas Conference on Information Systems*, San Diego, CA, p. 1760.

Zurko, M.E. 2020. "Cybersecurity Workforce Impacts of Technical Transition." Presentation to Committee on Cybersecurity Workforce of the Federal Aviation Administration. July 29, 2020. Virtual meeting.

5

Key Challenges and Opportunities

The Federal Aviation Administration (FAA) is responsible for providing the "safest, most efficient aerospace system in the world."[1] It has been significantly upgrading the technology used to manage aviation operations to increase the safety and efficiency of the National Airspace System (NAS). However, the modern computing and communications systems being introduced by the FAA, out of necessity magnify the cybersecurity threats to the NAS and its constituents, thereby providing a greater attack surface for criminals, terrorists, or nation-states to exploit. The FAA takes this seriously, recognizing that the consequences of this increasing digitization and connectivity without adequate cybersecurity could be enormous: disruption anywhere in the aviation sector can spread across borders, cause significant financial damages, and compromise safety.

Securing the computers, networks, and data that underpin modern aviation depends in part on the FAA having enough cybersecurity professionals (**capacity**) with the right knowledge, skills, and abilities (**capability**). It also depends on the FAA's workforce having sufficient **diversity** of backgrounds and experience. Diversity is critical in analyzing cybersecurity problems and is widely understood to be a "functional imperative" for effective cybersecurity programs (Levine, et. al., 2014). The future safety and security of air travel will rely, in part, on the ability of the FAA to build a workforce capable of addressing the evolving cybersecurity threat landscape.

Members of the committee represented expertise in related topical areas such as human capital management, industrial-organizational psychology, workforce diversity, industrial and systems engineering, and cybersecurity. Industry expertise was reflected in members who formerly served as senior managers of cybersecurity organizations, and government expertise was provided by a former deputy assistant administrator at the FAA.

The findings, conclusions, and recommendations contained herein derive from the academic literature, data received from the FAA, the committee's professional expertise, and input collected at the committee's five public meetings. At these meetings, the committee sought to learn about challenges and best practices from government and private-sector enterprises alike. The committee considered challenges in other aviation enterprises (such as the European Union Aviation Safety Agency), major logistics and transportation corporations (such as UPS) and other government agencies (such as the Department of Education and the United States Coast Guard). The preceding chapters provide committee's analysis, supporting evidence, and detailed findings, conclusions, and recommendations.

---

[1] More information is available at https:/www.faa.gov/about/mission/.

KEY CHALLENGES

Challenge 1. Expansion of the FAA's digital footprint also increases vulnerability and risk, and so, increases the need for more robust cybersecurity due to these potential new threats. Cybersecurity is an essential element of fulfilling the agency's mission of ensuring safety in air travel. It has become a critical priority for the FAA, as risk is compounded by growing digitization and connectivity of the NAS and aviation sector. As alluded to above, the increasing digitization of aviation infrastructure, while necessary to improve FAA operations, also expands the attack surface of critical infrastructure and cyber-physical systems. This led the committee to conclude (Conclusion 2-2) that "the cyber landscape of the FAA is continuously evolving. Accordingly, the future FAA cybersecurity workforce will need to adapt in order to simultaneously support traditional enterprise infrastructure and security operation center needs, as well as provide subject matter expertise and program oversight of cybersecurity integration into all aspects of FAA's missions." The profusion of digital technologies and the growing threat surface to the FAA's systems and operations add to the challenge by multiplying the number of skills needed to effectively manage cybersecurity risk. As the committee found (Finding 3-1) in Chapter 3, "the complexity of challenges that cybersecurity professionals address requires a workforce with a diversity of experiences and cognitive approaches, making diversity a functional imperative of cyber operations."

Challenge 2. The cybersecurity labor market is highly competitive within the federal sector, nationally, and globally—and likely to become more so. Cybersecurity professionals are highly sought after, and competition among employers for the limited applicant pool is likely to grow more acute. Despite a multitude of initiatives to address the cybersecurity workforce imperative, the nation still faces a significant shortage of qualified cybersecurity professionals. In Chapter 2, the committee found (Finding 2-5) that "the pool of qualified cybersecurity talent is limited and recruitment challenges will persist." The demand for talent is particularly severe in the public sector, because federal agencies must compete with private-sector firms that often can provide better compensation. As the committee found in Chapter 3, one of the current FAA cybersecurity workforce challenges is difficulty competing with commercial entities that have higher compensation packages. Nevertheless, federal employers (Finding 3-4) are able to recruit and retain personnel with the critical skills needed to accomplish their missions, by offering "incentives, such as recruitment, relocation, and retention incentive payments; student loan repayments; annual leave enhancements; and scholarships" to attract the necessary talent.

The FAA's workforce challenge is further compounded by its need for employees to have a deep understanding of a highly specialized mission and technology infrastructure alongside an ability to defend against both cyber and security threats. This confluence of labor market trends and specialized knowledge required to fulfill the agency's mission presents a substantial challenge to an agency whose recruitment capabilities, as discussed in Chapter 3, are presently insufficient to identify and recruit cybersecurity personnel aligned with FAA mission compared to foreseeable future needs. Furthermore, the FAA will have to integrate cybersecurity professionals and cybersecurity practices into the agency's strong existing safety culture.

Challenge 3. The FAA faces a future wave of retirements in its cybersecurity workforce. Like many federal agencies, the FAA has a significant portion of employees who are or soon will be eligible for retirement. As discussed in Chapter 2 (Finding 2-2), the committee found that "a growing proportion of the cybersecurity workforce of the FAA is reaching retirement eligibility and, as a result, the agency is vulnerable to losing a significant portion of its cybersecurity workforce to retirement." This means that within a relatively short timeframe, the FAA may have to replace a significant portion of its cybersecurity workforce amidst increasing competition for talent and ensure that the agency can retain the highly specialized, mission-specific knowledge of its retiring cybersecurity workforce. The cybersecurity workforce will need to adapt to the agency's adoption of internet protocol connectivity and the imposition of zero-trust networking authentication mechanisms. Employee retirement, at the end of the employee lifecycle model, "offers organizations the opportunity to rethink organizational needs and required skill sets, which in turn helps refocus talent recruitment and the next iteration of the employee lifecycle" (Recommendation 4-4).

Challenge 4. To achieve greater diversity within the cybersecurity workforce and meet its future needs, the agency must make better use of existing programs that promote workforce diversity. In Chapter 2 (Finding 2-1), the committee determined that the FAA could do more to grow both female and minority representation in its cybersecurity workforce. While the agency is better than average with diversity workforce trends for women, it may be lagging behind with regard to underrepresented minorities. This is somewhat uncertain due to incomplete data that may not fully reflect the presence of all minority groups among the FAA's workforce. The FAA's diversity track record is on par with federal agencies and broader trends in terms of diversity in the workforce and its success in recruiting and retaining underrepresented minorities and women. But the FAA lags other parts of the federal government in taking advantage of existing programs for enhancing diversity. For instance, as discussed in Chapter 4, many federal agencies, but not the FAA, have developed institutional partnerships with Minority-Serving Institutions (MSIs), which "can both expand the talent pool for high-demand positions and ensure diversity in the workforce for the long term" (Finding 4-3).

Increased diversity is vital to the FAA's future cybersecurity workforce for several reasons:

- Cybersecurity as a discipline incorporates a broad range of skills and knowledge, and thus an effective cybersecurity workforce will need to be diverse across a number of axes—a consideration that includes both traditional diversity strategies such as increased engagement of underrepresented minorities and women, and other strategies such as encouraging applicants from a range of different educational institutions, previous employers, and geographic locations.
- Greater diversity represents an opportunity to grow the talent pool and anticipate changing national demographics. Growing this talent pool will allow the FAA to keep pace with other organizations that have made diversity a recruitment priority.
- Adversaries present a changing set of threat activities that challenge the imagination. To manage these tactics, a diverse and multiview cyber defense is required as a critical part of the workforce.

Challenge 5. The FAA's current recruitment capabilities are not robust enough to meet future demand in an increasingly competitive environment. The FAA will need to be more effective in recruiting a cyber workforce of sufficient capability and capacity in the face of worldwide competition for cybersecurity talent, the need to be ready to replace a wave of retirees, and the need for greater diversity in its cybersecurity workforce. As noted above in Challenge 2 and in Chapter 4, the FAA has insufficient capabilities to identify and recruit cybersecurity personnel aligned with the FAA mission compared to foreseeable future needs. This includes insufficient engagement with existing sources of talent and organizational practices, each of which inhibits recruitment. For instance, the FAA has not partnered with universities to shape cybersecurity programs and curricula (Finding 3-10), a strategy that both provides students with the skills the agency anticipates needing in the future and builds relationships with faculty that can increase awareness of the FAA as an attractive employer for young cybersecurity professionals.

Additionally, the FAA does not take advantage of programs that other agencies use to recruit cybersecurity professionals into federal service (Finding 3-13), nor has it partnered with the Scholarship for Service program to effectively recruit cyber talent to the organization (Finding 3-9). While the agency's high retention rate among cybersecurity staff has thus far allowed for a relative lack of emphasis on identifying sources of new cybersecurity talent, this will need to become a higher operational priority as much of the cybersecurity workforce reaches retirement age.

Better organizational practices could help improve talent recruitment at the FAA. Even when talent is identified, FAA hiring practices can make the task of hiring in-demand cyber talent unnecessarily difficult, as the FAA is currently under-utilizing flexibilities in personnel management and hiring authority, such as direct-hire authority (Finding 2-6).

The challenges associated with building a diverse cybersecurity workforce of sufficient capability and capacity are in constant flux, and under particular pressure as the FAA expands its digital footprint. The opportunities summarized below and articulated in the previous chapters of this report provide some initial first steps that the FAA can take to strengthen its cybersecurity workforce.

KEY OPPORTUNITIES

Opportunity 1. Leverage the FAA's compelling mission as a recruitment tool. The FAA offers potential employees a work environment that combines cybersecurity operations with a unique mission (Finding 3-3). Through enhanced job fair materials, more compelling job descriptions, and engagements such as those identified in Opportunities 2-4, recruitment efforts can better highlight the opportunities to apply cybersecurity skills to the mission and within a unique operational environment (Finding 3-7).

Opportunity 2. Broaden the talent pipeline by building sustainable relationships with educational and industry partners and enhancing college recruitment. In order to help respond to the national imperative to grow the capability and capacity of the national and federal cybersecurity workforce and meet its own future needs, the FAA should consider investments in enriching educational curricula and scholarship programs and mining industry-based talent pools. Several federal agencies have developed successful, replicable partnership activities that provide research opportunities, scholar-in-residence positions for federal cybersecurity practitioners, and student internships. Successful engagement with these and similar programs can infuse the FAA with new cybersecurity talent. To realize this goal, the FAA will need to take full advantage of existing scholarship programs as well as explore new partnerships. The FAA should (1) evaluate the use of existing and future internship programs as a valuable tool to create a more diverse cybersecurity workforce (Recommendation 3-1); (2) organize and expand its reach and partnerships with universities around cybersecurity preparation efforts in academic and research areas in order to assist in the development of a talented cybersecurity workforce (Recommendation 3-3); and (3) set internal targets for the number of Scholarship for Service students recruited to internships and permanent positions within the agency (Conclusion 3-5).

Opportunity 3. Enhance diversity by leveraging existing best practices. Other federal agencies have developed best practices to improve workforce diversity. For instance, several agencies have developed partnerships with MSIs, similar to those discussed in Opportunity 2, that simultaneously attract young talent and improve organizational diversity. However, the FAA has not yet explored similar arrangements. To address this shortfall, the FAA can (1) explore opportunities to develop meaningful and sustainable relationships with MSIs to access upcoming cybersecurity graduates via internships and employment opportunities (Recommendation 3-3) and (2) train its cyber leadership on best practices in building a diverse and inclusive organizational culture (Recommendation 3-7).

Opportunity 4. Leverage federal hiring programs, nonsalary financial incentives, and flexibilities to attract and retain talent. Although subject to a number of requirements around federal hiring, the FAA could take better advantage of existing flexibilities, such as spot hiring authority (allowing employers to extend offers to qualified candidates without public posting requirements), that would allow it to more easily and nimbly recruit cyber talent. While the FAA, like other federal agencies, cannot realistically hope to match the salaries of private-sector employers, the agency can better use certain nonsalary incentives such as increased quality of work-life balance and targeted geographic opportunities to compete for talent more effectively with other federal agencies. The FAA should compare its use of hiring flexibilities with those of other federal agencies, both highlighting currently existing flexibilities that are underused by the FAA and identifying other agency flexibilities and practices that could be incorporated into FAA hiring processes (Recommendation 2-4).

Opportunity 5. Promote and invest in training and reskilling. Given the wide range of skills relevant to its cybersecurity practice, reskilling current employees—including current cybersecurity staff, non-cybersecurity information technology staff, and operations staff—can provide the FAA with a readily available talent pool of future cybersecurity talent. As the committee concluded, reskilling the existing workforce can be an important component of developing the needed future cybersecurity workforce of the FAA. To make best use of reskilling, the FAA should ensure that all efforts to upskill and evolve the cybersecurity workforce (Recommendation 3-5).

Opportunity 6. Anticipate the coming wave of retirements. The demographics of the FAA's cybersecurity workforce suggest that the agency will need to replace a significant portion of cybersecurity professionals in a relatively short timeframe. Although doing so will be challenging, the retirements also present an opportunity for FAA leadership to replace currently defined roles with ones that better reflect the future cybersecurity needs of the agency. To proactively address the challenges of anticipated retirements, the FAA should (1) implement cybersecurity workforce planning strategies that will protect the agency against the potential for sudden and mass retirements (Recommendation 2-1) and (2) provide professional development opportunities to refresh skill sets of current cybersecurity employees and ensure sharing of key institutional and mission-specific knowledge with newer cybersecurity staff (Recommendation 4-2).

Opportunity 7. Ensure that the FAA's CISO has sufficient authority and access to agency leadership. Mirroring private-sector trends that have bolstered the role of CISOs, the FAA should consider providing the CISO role with more authority and access to agency leadership, allowing the FAA to better identify and direct responses to cybersecurity challenges and foster an organizational culture in which cybersecurity professionals and other employees can be most effective in doing so. One option could be instituting a CISO's reporting structure to support a strong governance model, which ensures that the CISO has the independence and access required to effectively manage the FAA's cyber risk posture (Recommendation 4-3).

With this report, the committee hopes to provide FAA leadership with the information and tools necessary to ensure the continued success of the agency's cybersecurity workforce as it seeks a new generation of talent in an increasingly competitive market. The above opportunities represent a key subset of recommendations that, in the committee's estimation, will catalyze initial action toward meeting the prevailing challenges to the agency.

REFERENCE

Levine, S.S., Apfelbaum, E.P., Bernard, M., Bartelt, V.L., Zajac, E.J., and Stark, D. 2014. Ethnic diversity deflates price bubbles. *Proceedings of the National Academy of Sciences*, *111*(52), 18524–18529.

Appendixes

Appendix A

Committee Meeting Agendas

Committee on Cybersecurity Workforce of the Federal Aviation Administration
Meeting 1
February 19–20, 2020
The National Academies
2101 Constitution Avenue
Washington, D.C.

NAS 280

MEETING OBJECTIVES

- Conduct committee formation and member orientation to include the National Academies of Sciences, Engineering, and Medicine organization, procedures, and expectations of National Academies study committees
- Obtain consensus understanding, in consultation with the sponsor, on study scope
- Agree upon and baseline project plan, approach, and initial report outline
- Review topics and speakers for remaining meetings
- Obtain initial briefings containing information relevant to study issues
- Assign members to writing and fact-finding teams

Wednesday, February 19, 2020
CLOSED SESSION

7:30 a.m.–12:45 p.m.

OPEN SESSION

1:00 p.m. **Consensus Study Process for the Sponsor**
➢ Monica Feit, *Deputy Executive Director,* Division of Behavioral and Social Sciences and Education, The National Academies

1:25 p.m. **Committee Charge and Sponsor Expectations for Study**
➢ Larry Grossman, *Acting Director, Information Security & Privacy Service,* Federal Aviation Administration

5:15 p.m. Adjourn Meeting

CLOSED SESSION

5:45 p.m.–7:30 p.m.

Thursday, February 20. 2020

OPEN SESSION

7:30 a.m. **Review of Day 1 *with Breakfast Available***
➢ Tonya Smith-Jackson, *Co-Chair*
➢ Diana Burley, *Co-Chair*
➢ Daniel Talmage, *Co-Study Director*
➢ Brendan Roach, *Co-Study Director*

8:00 a.m. **Congressional Staffers Discussion**
➢ Invited

9:00 a.m. **Government Cyber Workforce Challenges**
➢ Steven Hernandez, *Chief Information Security Officer,* Department of Education

10:00 a.m. **Break**

10:15 a.m. **Industry Cyber Workforce Challenges**
➢ Alfred Lewis, *Senior Manager, Cyber Operations Center,* Boeing

11:15 a.m. **Sponsor Discussion**
➢ Larry Grossman, *Acting Director, Information Security & Privacy Service,* Federal Aviation Administration
➢ Tonya Smith-Jackson, *Co-Chair*
➢ Diana Burley, *Co-Chair*

END OF OPEN SESSION

CLOSED SESSION

12:15 p.m.–2:00 p.m.

APPENDIX A 85

Committee on Cybersecurity Workforce of the Federal Aviation Administration
Meeting 2
April 22–23, 2020

MEETING OBJECTIVES

- Obtain data-gathering briefings
- Determine topics and speakers for remaining meetings
- Identify locations for any individual site visits
- Discuss report progress and continue drafting report

Wednesday, April 22, 2020
CLOSED SESSION

9:30 a.m.–9:45 a.m.

OPEN SESSION

9:50 a.m. **Welcome**
- Tonya Smith-Jackson, *Co-Chair*
- Diana Burley, *Co-Chair*
- Daniel Talmage, *Co-Study Director*
- Brendan Roach, *Co-Study Director*

10:00 a.m. **Aviation Cybersecurity Workforce Challenges and Opportunities**
- Peter Cooper MSc FRAeS, *Chief Executive Officer*, Pavisade Cybersecurity

11:00 a.m. Committee Discussion with Participants

12:00 p.m. **Break**

BREAK FOR LUNCH

OPEN SESSION

1:00 p.m. **CyberCorps®: Developing Cybersecurity Workforce for Government Organizations**
- Victor Piotrowski, *Lead Program Director, CyberCorps,* National Science Foundation

2:00 p.m. **Cybersecurity Education and Workforce Perspectives from the National Initiative for Cybersecurity Education (NICE)**
- Rodney Petersen, *Director of the National Initiative for Cybersecurity Education (NICE),* National Institute of Standards and Technology

3:00 p.m. **Adjourn Meeting**

Thursday, April 23, 2020

OPEN SESSION

10:00 a.m. **The Cybersecurity Imperative**
- Steven Cook, *Visiting Research Scholar-in-Residence (CREO)*, North Carolina A&T State University

11:00 a.m. **Towards Gender Balance in Cybersecurity**
- Ambareen Siraj, *Professor*, Tennessee Tech; *Founder*, Women in Cybersecurity

12:00 p.m. **Break**

BREAK FOR LUNCH

OPEN SESSION

1:00 p.m. **Raytheon Cyber and Aviation Security**
- Michael Worden, *Chief Engineer, Cyber Operations*, Raytheon
- Heather Romero, *Technical Area Director for Cybersecurity*, Raytheon

2:00 p.m. **Sponsor Discussion**
- Larry Grossman, *Acting Director, Information Security & Privacy Service*, Federal Aviation Administration
- Ahmed Hussein, *Division Manager, Information Security & Privacy Governance*, Federal Aviation Administration

3:00 p.m. **Adjourn Meeting**

END OF OPEN SESSION

CLOSED SESSION

3:15 p.m.–5:00 p.m.

APPENDIX A

Committee on Cybersecurity Workforce of the Federal Aviation Administration
Meeting 3
June 29–30, 2020

MEETING OBJECTIVES

- Obtain data-gathering briefings
- Determine topics and speakers for remaining meetings
- Identify locations for any individual site visits
- Discuss report progress and continue drafting report

Monday, June 29, 2020
CLOSED SESSION

9:30 a.m.	**Open Closed Session**
9:45 a.m.	**Adjourn Closed Session**

OPEN SESSION

9:50 a.m.	**Welcome**
	➢ Tonya Smith-Jackson, *Co-Chair*
	➢ Diana Burley, *Co-Chair*
	➢ Daniel Talmage, *Co-Study Director*
	➢ Brendan Roach, *Co-Study Director*
10:00 a.m.	**Federal Perspectives: United States Coast Guard**
	➢ Commander Jamie Embry, *Cyberspace Planning and Resources Division*, Office of Cyberspace Forces, United States Coast Guard
11:00 a.m.	**Continuing Discussion**
12:00 p.m.	**Break**

BREAK FOR LUNCH

OPEN SESSION

1:00 p.m.	**Perspectives from Industry: UPS**
	➢ Juan Perez, *Chief Information and Engineering Officer*, UPS
2:00 p.m.	**Building an Evidence-Based Diversity and Inclusion Strategy**
	➢ Gail Greenfield, *Principal*, Mercer Consulting
3:00 p.m.	**AI and the Future of the Cybersecurity Workforce**
	➢ Frederick R. Chang (NAE), *Professor and Chair*, Computer Science Department, *Founding Director*, the Darwin Deason Institute for Cyber Security, Southern Methodist University
4:00 p.m.	**Adjourn Meeting**

Tuesday, June 30, 2020

OPEN SESSION

10:00 a.m. **Cybersecurity in Aviation: International Perspectives on Challenges and Workforce**
- Patrick Mana, *Program Manager*, EATM-CERT, Eurocontrol

11:00 a.m. **Airport Perspectives**
- Dominic Nessi, *former CISO*, Los Angeles International Airport

12:00 p.m. **Break**

BREAK FOR LUNCH

OPEN SESSION

1:00 p.m. **Building a Diverse Workforce**
- Mauricio Velasquez, *President*, Diversity Training Group

2:00 p.m. **Sponsor Discussion**
- Larry Grossman, *Acting Director, Information Security & Privacy Service*, Federal Aviation Administration
- Ahmed Hussein, *Division Manager, Information Security & Privacy Governance*, Federal Aviation Administration

3:00 p.m. **Adjourn Meeting**

END OF OPEN SESSION

CLOSED SESSION

3:15 p.m. **Open Closed Session**

5:00 p.m. **Adjourn Meeting**

APPENDIX A   89

Committee on Cybersecurity Workforce of the Federal Aviation Administration
Meeting 4
July 29–30, 2020

MEETING OBJECTIVES

- Obtain data-gathering briefings
- Determine topics and speakers for remaining meetings
- Identify personnel of interest for any individual site visits
- Discuss report progress and continue drafting report

Wednesday, July 29, 2020
CLOSED SESSION

9:30 a.m.	**Open Closed Session**
9:45 a.m.	**Adjourn Closed Session**

OPEN SESSION

9:50 a.m. **Welcome**
- Tonya Smith-Jackson, *Co-Chair*
- Diana Burley, *Co-Chair*
- Daniel Talmage, *Co-Study Director*
- Brendan Roach, *Co-Study Director*

10:00 a.m. **Cybersecurity Workforce Impacts of Technical Transition**
- Mary Ellen Zurko, *Technical Staff Member*, Lincoln Lab

11:00 a.m. **FAA Office of Civil Rights Briefing**
- Sadie Perez, *Deputy Director*, National Outreach Team for Diversity and Inclusion, Office of Civil Rights, FAA

12:00 p.m. **Break**

BREAK FOR LUNCH

OPEN SESSION

1:00 p.m. **The Future of the FAA: Medium- and Long-Term Horizons**
- Larry Grossman, *Acting Chief Information Security Officer*, FAA

2:00 p.m. **Risk Management and Cybersecurity Strategy for Federal Agencies**
- Earl Crane, *Professor*, Carnegie Mellon University

3:00 p.m. **Labor Relations and the Cybersecurity Workforce**
- Patricia Gilbert, *Executive Vice President*, NATCA

4:00 p.m. **Adjourn Session**

Thursday, July 30, 2020

CLOSED SESSION

10:00 a.m. **Open Closed Session**

10:45 a.m. **Adjourn Closed Session**

OPEN SESSION

11:00 a.m. **Future of Cybersecurity**
- Gilman Louie, *Partner*, Alsop Louie Partners

12:00 p.m. **Break**

BREAK FOR LUNCH

OPEN SESSION

1:00 p.m. **Designing Business and Cybersecurity Strategy into Cybersecurity Operating and Organizational Models**
- Charlie Lewis, *Expert Associate Partner,* McKinsey and Company

2:00 p.m. **Establishing Foundations of Human Performance in Industrial Cybersecurity**
- Dr. Shane Stailey, *Senior Industrial Control Systems Cybersecurity Professional*, Idaho National Laboratory
- Dr. Sean McBride, *Industrial Cybersecurity Program Coordinator,* Idaho State

3:00 p.m. **Adjourn Open Session**

END OF OPEN SESSION

CLOSED SESSION

3:15 p.m. **Open Closed Session**

5:00 p.m. **Adjourn Meeting**

APPENDIX A

Committee on Cybersecurity Workforce of the Federal Aviation Administration
Meeting 5
September 15–16, 2020

MEETING OBJECTIVES

- Obtain data-gathering briefings
- Determine topics and speakers for remaining meetings
- Identify personnel of interest for any individual site visits
- Discuss report progress and continue drafting report

Tuesday, September 15, 2020

CLOSED SESSION

9:30 a.m.	**Open Closed Session**
9:45 a.m.	**Adjourn Closed Session**

OPEN SESSION

9:50 a.m. **Welcome**
- Tonya Smith-Jackson, *Co-Chair*
- Diana Burley, *Co-Chair*
- Daniel Talmage, *Co-Study Director*
- Brendan Roach, *Co-Study Director*

10:00 a.m. **Best Practices for Robust Cyber Organizations**
- Samuel Visner, *Director*, National Cybersecurity Federally Funded Research Center

11:00 a.m. **DOT Human Capital Programs**
- Anne Audet, *Deputy Director*, Departmental Office of Human Resource Management, Department of Transportation

12:00 p.m. **Summary of Site Visits**
- Eric Grosse, *Committee Member*

12:15 p.m. **Break**

BREAK FOR LUNCH

CLOSED SESSION

1:00 p.m. **Open Closed Session**

5:00 p.m. **Adjourn Closed Session**

Wednesday, September 16, 2020

OPEN SESSION

10:00 a.m. **Recruiting Mission-Critical Cyber Personnel**
- Rick Kempinski, *Senior Manager*, Federal Workforce, Partnership for Public Service
- Lucy Cunningham, *Senior Manager*, Federal Workforce, Partnership for Public Service

11:00 a.m. **Attracting Young Cyber Talent to the Federal Workforce**
- Leisel Bogan, *Director*, Congressional Digital Service Fellowship

12:00 p.m. **Break**

BREAK FOR LUNCH

CLOSED SESSION

1:00 p.m. **Open Closed Session**

4:45 p.m. **Adjourn Closed Session and Meeting**

Appendix B

Committee Biosketches

Tonya L. Smith-Jackson (*Co-Chair*) is senior vice provost for academic affairs and professor of industrial and systems engineering at North Carolina A&T State University. She is the founder and director of the Human Factors Analytics Laboratory, founder and co-director of the Cyber-Human Analytics Research for the Internet-of-Things Laboratory, and former program director in the Computer and Information Science and Engineering Directorate of the National Science Foundation. She is a fellow of the Human Factors and Ergonomics Society and the Institute of Industrial and Systems Engineers, American Society of Engineering Education. She is certified by the Board of Certification in professional ergonomics and by the National Science Foundation for personnel security and suitability. Her work has focused on ensuring processes, analytic methods, and technologies are equitable and inclusive across cultures, genders, abilities, and generations. Smith-Jackson has a B.A. in psychology from the University of North Carolina at Chapel Hill, an interdisciplinary M.S. in industrial engineering and psychology, and a Ph.D. in psychology/ergonomics from North Carolina State University.

Diana L. Burley (*Co-Chair*) is vice provost for research at American University (AU) where she is also professor of public administration and policy in the School of Public Affairs and professor of information technology and analytics in the Kogod School of Business. Burley is an expert on cybersecurity, information sharing, and digital transformation who advises members of Congress, corporate executives, academic institutions, and government agencies around the world on building workforce capacity, managing enterprise risk, and strengthening cybersecurity posture. Prior to AU, she was professor of human and organizational learning at the George Washington University and director of its Institute for Information Infrastructure Protection (I3P); previously, she was a program officer at the National Science Foundation, where she led the CyberCorps program. In 2018, she led the Joint Task Force on Cybersecurity Education that published the first set of global cybersecurity curricular guidelines for postsecondary academic institutions. Burley is a member of the U.S. National Academies Board on Human-Systems Integration and on the research staffs of the Idaho National Laboratory and the Johns Hopkins University Applied Physics Laboratory. She has been honored by the U.S. Federal CIO Council and the Colloquium for Information Systems Security Education (as the sole recipient of both educator of the year and government leader of the year awards). She holds a B.A. in economics from the Catholic University of America, and an M.S. in public management and policy, an M.S. in organization science, and a Ph.D. in organization science and information technology from Carnegie Mellon University, where she was a Woodrow Wilson Foundation fellow.

Rodney C. Adkins (NAE) is chairman of Avnet, Inc., a Fortune 500 company and one of the world's largest distributors of electronic components and embedded solutions. In addition, he is president of 3RAM Group LLC, a privately held company specializing in capital investments, business consulting services, and property management. Formerly, Adkins was senior vice president of IBM, having served in that position from 2007 until 2014. In his more than 33-year career, Adkins has held a number of operational and executive management roles spanning across strategy, technology, systems, and supply chain. Adkins was inducted into the National Academy of Engineering (NAE) in 2005. He serves on the board of directors for United Parcel Service (UPS), PayPal, Grainger, and Avnet. He is a member of the Executive Leadership Council (ELC), and a trustee of the Georgia Institute of Technology (Georgia Tech) and Rollins College. Adkins also serves on the UMBC Board of Visitors and the Adrienne Arsht Center Trust Board. He previously served on the boards of PPL Corporation, Pitney Bowes, PeopleClick Inc., the National Action Council for Minorities in Engineering, the Kappa Alpha Psi Foundation, the Harlem School of the Arts, and the Smithsonian National Board. Adkins holds a B.S. and M.S. in electrical engineering from Georgia Tech, as well as a B.A. with an emphasis in physics from Rollins College.

Jandria S. Alexander is a vice president at Booz Allen Hamilton where she leads cybersecurity and research and development, and serves as chief technology officer. She is a subject matter expert on cybersecurity, resilient platform, operational technology, and multidomain mission systems with more than 20 years in the field. A nationally recognized cybersecurity expert, Alexander has participated in National Academy of Sciences studies related to cybersecurity research and new aviation technologies. In 2014, she was appointed by former Virginia Governor Terry McAuliffe to serve on the bipartisan Virginia Cyber Security Commission to expand the state's economic footprint in cyber technology and protect critical infrastructure from cyber threats. She led the effort's unmanned systems cybersecurity industry, government, and academia consortium. Over the length of her career, Alexander has provided cybersecurity and digital transformation leadership, market strategy, and solution development for the Department of Defense and the intelligence community as well as many civil and commercial organizations. Before joining Booz Allen in 2017, she was a cybersecurity leader in engineering and technology at a federally funded research and development corporation. She served as the chair of the American Association of Aeronautics and Astronautics' Diversity and Inclusion Working Group from 2017 to 2021. She has a B.S. in computer science from Brandeis University and an M.S. in technology management from American University.

Marilyn Barrios is the head of application security at Motorola Solutions, where she works on creating, implementing, and driving security strategies relevant to secure software development lifecycle, secure coding best practices, cybersecurity testing, tooling, and automation across all products and development groups. Her previous roles at Motorola included global cybersecurity manager where she worked on human resources strategies for Motorola's cyber workforce as well as integrating new employees and developing cyber strategies for personnel across the organization. Prior positions at Motorola Solutions included leading their Cybersecurity Training & Awareness program. She brings relevant experience in safety from working within Motorola's law enforcement and first responder communities as well as experience in understanding labor and cyber projections. She has also served as an adjunct faculty member at the College of DuPage, where she teaches courses for the STEM program in the department of youth education. In addition, Barrios serves as a coach and mentor for the United States Air Force CyberPatriot program. Barrios holds a master's in computer and information security from the Illinois Institute of Technology and has more than 10 years of IT sales management experience.

Charles Blauner is a partner and chief information security officer (CISO) in residence at Team8 Ventures and a venture advisor at the Cyber Mentors Fund. Blauner is also the president of Cyber Aegis, a boutique cyber risk management consultancy. He has worked in information security for more than 30 years, 25 of which were in financial services; previous positions include the CISO at JP Morgan and Deutsche Bank and the global head of information security at Citi. During this time, Blauner also served as chair of the Financial Services Sector Coordinating Council, founding director of the Financial Services Information Sharing and Analysis Center, and the chair of the OpenGroup's Security Program. He has worked closely with banking regulators around the world (OCC, FRB, BoE, MAS, and HKMA) to help reduce the risk posed by cyber threats to the financial sector at large.

Blauner has appeared in front of U.S. House and Senate committees. In 2015, he received the Joseph J. Wasserman Award from the Information Systems Audit and Control Association, New York Metropolitan Chapter. Blauner has an M.S. in computer science from the University of Southern California and a B.S. in computer science from Rensselaer Polytechnic Institute.

Michael D. Coovert is professor emeritus of industrial-organizational psychology at the University of South Florida (USF). Coovert's research includes the impact of technology on individuals and organizations to job analysis, human-robot interaction, and quantitative analysis. Through his consulting firm (MDC & Associates), he has focused on performance of individuals in cyber occupations, particularly on cognitive and noncognitive predictors of performance for cyber occupations (enlisted and officer) in the U.S. Air Force. Coovert was also the founding director of The Institute for Human Performance, Decision Making, and Cybernetics at USF from 1992 to 2013. His research has been supported by the Department of Defense, the U.S. Army, U.S. Navy, and U.S. Air Force. Honors include the Illinois State University Department of Psychology's Award for Lifetime Career Achievement; the University of South Florida Presidential Award; and elected Fellow of The Society for Industrial and Organizational Psychology, American Psychological Association, and Association for Psychological Science. He is a Federal Aviation Administration-certified pilot for single engine land aircraft and holds an instrument rating. Coovert received his Ph.D. in psychology from The Ohio State University with an emphasis in industrial and organizational with doctoral minor work in computer science.

Barbara Endicott-Popovsky is executive director and principal research scientist of the Center for Information Assurance, an NSA/DHS Center of Academic Excellence in Cyber Defense Education and Research affiliate professor at University of Washington (UW) Bothell's department of computer science and systems and UW Seattle's Department of Urban Planning and Management; and a faculty appointment at University of Hawaii Manoa's department of information and computer science. She was named department fellow at Aberyswyth University Wales in 2012. Her academic career follows a 20-year career at the Boeing Company marked by executive and consulting positions in IT architecture and project management. Her research interests include information assurance, enterprise-wide information systems security and compliance management, forensic-readiness, cybersecurity education, secure coding practices, and addressing the worldwide talent gap in cybersecurity professionals. For her work in the relevance of archival sciences to digital forensics, she was named a fellow of the American Academy of Forensic Scientists. She holds a Ph.D. in computer science/computer security from University of Idaho's Center for Secure and Dependable Systems, an M.S. in information systems engineering from Seattle Pacific University, an M.B.A. from the University of Washington, and a B.A. from the University of Pittsburgh.

Eric Grosse retired from Google as vice president of security and privacy engineering, where his team achieved improved and wider use of SSL, stronger consumer authentication technology, detection and blocking of espionage, transparency on legal requests for data, and sophisticated malware analysis, and built tools and frameworks for safer web applications. Before Google, Grosse was a research director and fellow at Lucent Bell Labs, where he worked on security, networking, algorithms for approximation and visualization, software distribution, and scientific computing. Currently, he builds open systems and advises companies on security. He has a Ph.D. in computer science from Stanford University and is also an instrument-rated private pilot.

Robert S. Gutzwiller is an assistant professor at Arizona State University, where he studies the critical role of the human in complex systems. His work scientifically applies cognitive engineering to health care, cyberspace, transportation, and defense. His recent research focuses on studying and engineering attention, human-automation interaction (How do humans learn to interact with complex systems, particularly those which use automation, artificial intelligence, and machine learning?), and defensive cyberspace operations (How does a cyber analyst protecting networks develop awareness? Could properties of attention be used against would-be attackers to make defenses more robust?). Gutzwiller has been funded and worked on projects for the Army Research Office, Assistant Secretary of Defense, the Defense Advanced Research Projects Agency, the National Aeronautics and Space Administration, and the Office of Naval Research, among others. Gutzwiller has been recognized for exceptional leadership and mentoring across several multidisciplinary engineering projects in cyberspace and ship defense systems, receiving leadership and exemplary achievement awards from the U.S. Navy in 2017 and 2018. Gutzwiller holds a Ph.D. in cognitive psychology from Colorado State University.

Katya Le Blanc is a senior human factors scientist who has been conducting research in the energy sector at Idaho National Laboratory for 10 years. Her research in nuclear power plant modernization has led transformational change in the way field operators conduct procedures and has improved operator interfaces for control of nuclear power plant equipment in the field and in the control room. She has led design of human-system interfaces for transmission system technologies and cybersecurity for electric grid operation. She leads research in several complex, multidisciplinary subjects including nuclear power plant modernization and cybersecurity risk characterization in nuclear power and critical infrastructure, and is the deputy national technical director of the cybersecurity program for the Department of Energy's office of Nuclear Energy. She has also conducted research investigating the characteristics of highly skilled cybersecurity professionals to develop insights for cybersecurity workforce development and education. LeBlanc has more than 100 technical publications in the subject of human factors in the energy sector. She is a senior member of IEEE, and holds a Ph.D. and master's in cognitive psychology from New Mexico State and a B.S. in psychology from New Mexico Institute of Mining and Technology.

Nan Shellabarger is the previous acting deputy assistant administrator for policy, international affairs, and environment for the Federal Aviation Administration (FAA). In this role, she led the agency's efforts to increase the safety and capacity of the global aerospace system in an environmentally sound manner. This includes leading the FAA strategic policy and planning efforts; coordinating the agency's reauthorization before Congress; overseeing the national and international aviation policies, strategies, and research efforts in the environment and energy arenas; and managing the FAA's aviation activity forecasts, economic analyses, and regulatory evaluations. Prior to that assignment, Shellabarger had been the executive director for policy and plans at the FAA. In this role, she was responsible for setting direction and overseeing operations for the FAA's policy organization. That office is responsible for providing economic and policy analysis and planning services for issues that cover the entire FAA. She holds an M.B.A. and a B.S. from the University of Michigan, as well as a private pilot certificate with an instrument rating.